bring the joy

bring the joy

how following
the nudges of your heart leads
to an abundant life

JESSICA JANZEN

Fedd Books
P.O. Box 341973
Austin, TX 78734

www.thefeddagency.com

Published in association with The Fedd Agency, Inc., a literary agency.

Scripture quotations marked (KJV) are taken from the King James Version
of the Bible.

Scripture quotations marked (MSG) are taken from THE MESSAGE,
copyright © 1993, 1994, 1995, 1996, 2000, 2001, 2002 by Eugene H. Pe-
terson. Used by permission of NavPress. All rights reserved. Represented by
Tyndale House Publishers, Inc.

ISBN: 978-1-949784-41-1
eISBN: 978-1-949784-42-8

Library of Congress Control Number: 2020903559

Printed in Canada.

Second Edition 21 22 23 24 / 10 9 8 7 6 5 4 3

To anyone who is in or has been in the darkness.

There is light, there is hope, but most importantly, there is joy.

The joy is coming.

Just keep responding to the nudges on your heart.

TABLE OF CONTENTS

Introduction: The Nudges 9

1. An Orange Plastic Chair 15
2. Fresh Start 23
3. Change Of Heart 31
4. Value Village Meets Holt Renfrew...............................39
5. Hot Ronnie 47
6. The Spanish Lover..57
7. Are You Ok?...63
8. Leap Of Faith 73
9. Crying In Trailers And Kissing On Cars.......................87
10. Falling In Love And Falling Apart 95
11. The Parking Lot 105
12. Stubborn In Love 119
13. Oh Baby 129
14. The Diagnosis 137
15. The Pact 149
16. A Used Baby Book 157
17. Fight For Lewiston's Life 165
18. Not Getting The Miracle 175
19. Leave The Chili At Home 181
20. Love For Lewiston...199
21. Easy As Platz 205

Conclusion: Chips All In..217

THE NUDGES

Have you ever been going about your business, and out of nowhere, you feel a nudge deep inside you? You know, it tugs at you, stirs your heart, and aches in your belly? That same thought comes up in your head over and over again? The nudge could be anything from suddenly wanting to rearrange all the furniture in your bedroom to texting your husband to tell him you love him and think he's really hot. Or the nudge could be to go back to school and get the degree that you have always wanted, or to move across the country without really knowing what you're going to do once you get there. Or the nudge could be to start the business, the podcast, the YouTube channel.

This book is about those nudges—big and small. I believe these deep-seated nudges are holy, even sacred. I believe they are a pathway to experience and live in incredible joy.

When I say these nudges are sacred, I don't mean that in a holier-than-thou way, like I have some mystical, transcendent life. (Just look at the current state of my office, and you'll immediately know there's nothing transcendent about my life.) In all transparency, some of my nudges have been crazy like: going to Costa Rica to visit a boy I'd known for two months (and we only knew each other mostly through Skype . . .), quitting my job with a six-figure salary selling software, and deciding to move to a new city just for the hell of it. These moments were not necessarily sacred in and of themselves (although, at the time, I did think my love for Carlitos was pretty heavenly). But what these moments brought—the path of joy they left in their wake and the person I became from following the nudges—that, my friends, is sacred. Following those nudges is truly living on purpose.

You might attribute these nudges to a different source than I do. For me, I believe these nudges have always come from God, and it is His plan for me that brings joy. Whether you believe the nudges are from yourself, your spirit, God, the universe, a higher power, or the voice of someone you love doesn't really matter. What does matter, however, is that you learn to follow the path of joy, and I truly believe that these nudges are leading you there.

The nudges we get lead us to a choice. We can either choose to follow them and live a life of abundant and steadfast joy, or we can choose to go our own way and do what is comfortable, which will ultimately lead to dissatisfaction. When you decide to lead a life of joy, it will not be easy; it comes with pain, honest conversations, and perseverance. Trust me, I know. I have been knocked down so many dang times. But I also know that by getting back up, rising again and again, and following through on those nudges is always worth it.

This book walks you through how my life forever changed when I truly started paying attention to and acting on those nudges. From the bliss of the dramatic and romantic saga with my now husband, to the trials and triumph of my career journey as a young woman, to the devastating loss of my son, my story in these pages will not shy away from the highest highs and the lowest lows.

I lost my son Lewiston just three days shy of his six-month birthday. If you have ever experienced loss of any kind, you know how brutal it is. Watching Lewiston take his last breaths was the worst day of my life. Yet now, I can truthfully say that I have experienced more joy and discovered a deeper capacity for joy in myself through witnessing his short life. Losing Lewiston changed me, and I just knew I had to share our story. I guess you could say I was nudged to do so. And so, after years of procrastinating and allowing doubt, fear, and all of the stupid voices that say you're not good enough to win, I finally kicked it all to the curb. I showed up, stayed consistent, and did the hard work. I sat in coffee shops, hotel lounges, and my home office and finally finished this book so that I could share my story with you. So that I could share the nudges that led to deep-rooted joy. Because truth be told, I believe the world would be a much better place if we brought joy to all we did, even when it means bringing joy in the face of death.

Not a day goes by without thanking the Lord for the days I got to spend with Lewiston. Not a day goes by where I don't recall his smile, his big blue eyes, and our dance parties. He lit up the room with his bright eyes and his captivating smile—just like his dad.

Lewiston's life was—and still is—an amazing display of hope. If he made his life count with only 179 days, why can't we do the same? They say the average person gets 30,000 days. When my family's world was rocked by one single conversation, a terminal diagnosis, the 30,000 days we figured our son would have quickly became less than 365. And even still, Lewiston touched lives. He fought. He inspired epic dance parties. He brought countless people closer to God and encouraged them to make their days count. Truly, there were so many miracles in his one little life, and there still are.

Don't get me wrong, I am still grieving. I will always be grieving the loss of my son Lewiston, but the joy of knowing him and seeing the impact that he had on the earth in such a short time makes the grief a little easier to swallow. The joy makes the sting of loss a little less painful. In a weird way, the joy makes all the crap worth it. In the midst of my sorrow and hurt, in the midst of my questions and confusion and even chaos, I learned to trust God's heart even when it was hard to see His plan. Because let's be honest—losing my son was not in my plan. Trust me.

God nudged me and my husband to walk through this journey joyfully. Following that nudge has led me to immeasurable joy and memories I will hold dear for the rest of my life. You see, we get to choose how we respond to the cards we are dealt. Ronnie noted at Lewiston's funeral that AN EVENT + YOUR REACTION = YOUR OUTCOME. For our family, we chose to respond with dance parties. Yep. When facing death, we chose more dance parties and less pity parties.

If you take just one thing away from this book, I want it to be this: learn to follow the promptings and whispers of your heart; learn to listen to those nudges. They are there for a reason. My prayer is that you will rise up and go after whatever that nudge might be. Stop complaining and sitting idle. Stop wasting the hours, minutes, and seconds you have been given. Stop being so busy that you miss out on the amazing things right in front of you. Stop answering how you're doing with "Busy. I'm so busy." Busyness is not the state of your heart. Busyness is a by-product of how you planned (or didn't plan) your day, week, or year. Turn off the TV, stop scrolling and watching other people's accomplishments that make you jealous, and take action. You have breath in your lungs and a beating heart. You have dreams and goals and ideas that are too good to slip away. I hope my story encourages you to wake up, pay attention, and get going! Follow the nudges and trust that they will bring you some of your biggest blessings. Yes, those silly little nudges will be your biggest blessings!

My hope for you, as you read this, is that you go all in. As you turn the pages and read about my journey and all of the challenges and blessings in my life, I hope you will trust your heart and follow those nudges as well. My prayer is that you would follow the simple nudges, like holding open the door for that elderly lady, or making eye contact and smiling at the stranger passing by. The nudge to go visit the friend that's been on your heart for weeks, to pray for that person when he comes to mind, or to give away the shirt that you spent hard-earned money on but makes your bestie smile from ear to ear. The nudge to bring a coworker to church, to be bold, to quit the job that isn't right, set a goal and actually do it, run a marathon, tell your best friend you're in love with them (and then tell them three more times until they get the picture). Chase after what excites you, what moves you. Travel, explore, dream bigger. My charge is that you would do all of those things. And do them with joy.

I'm cheering for you more than you know.

With love and the deepest thanks for pickin' up a copy and at least reading this far. I hope you enjoy this nudge to keep reading.

xo —

jess

AN ORANGE PLASTIC CHAIR

the nudge to identify the love story you want

I really understood love when my grandma gave my grandpa a piece of pie.

Ok, there's a bit more to the story than just the hand off of pie. In 2005, my grandpa got sick and found out he was dying of cancer. The cancer was weakening his body, and at times, it was unbearable to watch. I am sure far too many of you reading this have been affected by that cursed word—cancer. It a real mother F'er. (Oh yes, there will be some language used in this book. My therapist says it's okay. Sometimes, a curse word is truly the only way to describe the horrific crap, trauma, and pain we go through. Sorry Mom, my pastors, and anyone else that is offended. Skim over the language, and keep reading.)

My grandma spent most of her life being driven around by my grandpa. She wasn't comfortable driving around the city on her own, so on that particular day in 2005, I volunteered to pick her up to go and visit Grandpa at the hospital. We headed to the hospital together and walked through the dark halls to his room. The smell of "hospital" was extra strong that day. Patients were roaming the halls with butt cheeks exposed, and medical supplies lined the halls. We got into Grandpa's room, and I decided to give my grandparents a moment.

I am not sure why, but I sat quietly that day in the only chair in the corner of the room—a bright orange plastic chair. I don't often just sit, and rarely am I quiet. If you have met me in person, you know this almost never happens. But in the moment, something nudged me to just be quiet and watch.

My grandma was standing across from Grandpa Plett at his bedside. She said, "Peter, I snuck you in some platz." Platz is a Mennonite form of fruit pie, which I know because, fun fact, I grew up Mennonite. (But my parents were pretty progressive and hip . . . you know, for Mennonites.)

"Thank you, Sue." He smiled up at her.

We have all seen *The Notebook*, right? Okay if not, you're crazy, go find it on Netflix or whatever streaming service it's on, and watch it now. Oh, and bring some tissues because it is a real tear-jerker. The quick version is that Noah meets Allie and knows that she is the one. Several obstacles come between them and their relationship, but Noah fights through and gets the girl. He spends his life loving his bride, making her feel cherished and like she's the only girl in the world. All the way to their deaths, they are in love like it was the first time they met. I cry every time I watch that movie—even though I know exactly what's going to happen. I just love watching their love story. And that day in the hospital, I saw a real-life version of that kind of love. Sixty-four years of a love story was right in front of me. It's crazy that it took me this long to notice.

Grandpa was just supposed to be on liquids only, as he was getting more treatment. But my grandparents didn't mind breaking the rules; he was dying, so why not enjoy life's simple pleasures in his last days. Here's the deal, my grandparents were not rule-breakers by any means. They did everything just so. If they owed someone money, they would pay them back to the penny. My grandma was so detailed and thorough that even at the age of eighty-nine, she was still helping others with their taxes and finding them ways to save money.

My grandpa swung his legs over the edge of his bed, my grandma rolled the hospital table over to him, and they opened up the homemade platz that was so carefully wrapped up in wax paper. Grandpa Plett then bowed his head to pray. I don't remember the words exactly, but it was in that moment that the course of my life changed forever.

He bowed his head and thanked God. Yes, in his weakness, in his dying, and with his failing body, he bowed his head and thanked God. Talk about an incredible gratitude practice.

In that bright orange plastic chair, I had a front row seat to witness the love that I truly wanted. The type of love that has stuck with me for a lifetime—the unconditional, life-long kind. The first love I saw is a love for Jesus. But the second is a love for a partner so true, so deep, it makes your heart ache.

I sat on that orange plastic chair and let the hot tears stream down my face. That moment will forever be etched into my brain. The platz, the crinkle of the wax paper, the feel of the orange plastic chair, my grandpa's pale skinny legs (I don't think those legs ever saw the sun), the tender moment of a deep-rooted marriage—all of it.

I decided right there that I wanted a marriage like that. I wanted sixty-four years of love and faithfulness, I wanted a partner who would sneak in platz when I was dying, that would come sit with me and laugh and pray and do crosswords. (Well, let's be honest, I have never done a crossword and probably never will, but you get the idea).

I also wanted a faith like that. A faith that gives thanks when life is so awful, when death is knocking at your door. When you have cancer, and your body is weak and crumbling. A faith that is thankful when it feels like you have nothing to be thankful for. I was blown away that in the midst of heartache and death, my grandpa could still give thanks.

I wanted to live a life like that. That even when everything sucks, you can still find a reason to give thanks and find joy in a piece of pie.

After we left the hospital, I made some changes. That moment *actually* affected me. And not just a little. It was enough to spark *real* change in my life.

Let me give you a picture of how I was living at that point in my life: I would listen to DMX and frequently go to gas stations to pick up cigarettes. Yep, I used to smoke for all of like two years or something like that. I lied to my parents when they asked why the car smelled like smoke. Silly me to think they wouldn't notice. I would drink Tim Hortons coffee (half French vanilla, half coffee), smoke, and play rap in my parents' massive white Chevy Suburban. If you have met me recently, you would laugh uncontrollably at this image. Because I don't touch Tim Hortons with a ten-foot pole, I think smoking is disgusting, and can only handle rap in very small doses, typically in a spin class.

But on that cold day in January 2005, I made a decision to change things around. I went through my car and got rid of all of my non-Christian music. I went to the Christian bookstore and bought books, a new Bible that was cool to carry around (as cool as possible for carrying around a big, ancient book), and got new CDs—yes, music streaming was not even a thing yet. I was bound and determined to make some positive changes and experience the kind of love and faith I saw in my grandparents.

After I made those changes, my nickname became the "Jesus Police" for a really long time. If you swore around me, I'd glare you down and then politely tell you that you shouldn't swear because it wasn't God-honouring. (Don't worry, I roll my eyes at that now.) I began attending church more regularly and told my boyfriend at the time that some changes needed to be made in our relationship, seeing as we were having sex at the time. That didn't go over so well. It was tough, and things kind of went sideways. But I stood firm in my belief and conviction to really change.

On June 11, 2005, I was baptized at the church our family attended. I publicly declared that I wanted other people to know that I followed Jesus.

If my heart had not been nudged that day to drive my grandma to the hospital, I would have sat at home and may have missed one of the most life changing moments ever. Can you imagine if I said I was too busy or didn't want to go because I was going to "chill at home"? In watching my grandfather's life, I got one of the wakeup calls I needed to press into some big decisions and take steps in the right direction. The nudge to take my grandma to the hospital wasn't groundbreaking; driving with her in my car didn't revolutionize my life. But in listening to that nudge and following my gut, I became aware of a deeper capacity for love than I'd ever known before.

When we find an example of the kind of love we want, we can begin the process of knowing we are worthy of that love. You, friend, are worthy of the love you crave. We were built for it. I know that we can make the practical changes we need to make in order to live in light of our known worth.

Watching my grandparents share a piece of smuggled-in pie led me to become the person I am today. It led me to a perfectly imperfect, crazy, and messy love story of my own that I wouldn't change for the world. It led me to a faith that's been tried and tried again. At the end of the day and amidst the hardest seasons, I still find myself on my knees, thanking and praising God, even when I don't understand His plan. Gratitude has become my way of life and my default setting!

When I think back to that day in the hospital, I always seem to fixate on my posture: sitting, listening, observing. In both trying and quiet moments, I try to mimic this posture—listening for those nudges, sitting firmly in gratitude, and observing all the joy that is happening around me—even in the face of loss and death. When I think of this posture, I think of the story of Mary and Martha in the Bible. Jesus came over to their house to hang out with them. Martha was preparing the charcuterie board (or the Bible-day equivalent) and trying to be the hostess with the mostest, while Mary sat with Jesus, listening to Him, observing Him and the joy and peace He carried. Martha got mad at Mary for not helping her (yeah, I would too). But Jesus said, "Don't worry so much, Martha. Mary's actually got her priorities straight" (Luke 10:41-42 paraphrased).

In this hyperactive world where busy equals success, I want to pause more and sit, listen, and observe—just like Mary. There is great joy to be found in sitting down, shutting up, and observing a powerful love— whether that is watching an old couple eat a piece of pie together, basking in the words and lessons of Jesus, or speaking kind words to yourself. Love is everywhere—and I don't mean that in a mushy, gushy Valentine's Day sense. I am talking about profound, unconditional, life-changing love. Loving deeply in this way and accepting this love from others brings joy. Other things in life bring happiness, euphoria, and bliss, which are a great deal of fun but innately fleeting. (Trust me, wait until we get to the chapter on my Costa Rican lover). But this kind of love that I observed from the orange plastic chair . . . that, my friends, brings joy—lasting, steadfast joy.

THE NUDGE:

Recall the purest form of love you've ever seen. It could be from a book or movie; it could be from real life. Between a parent and child, between a husband and wife, between two strangers. Imagine it in all its vivid detail. And know that you are worthy of that kind of love, truly and inherently worthy.

THE CHOICE:

When it comes to accepting unconditional, profound, and life-changing love, it can often be difficult to see ourselves as worthy of that love. What have we done to deserve this? We haven't done anything and we can't do anything; that's the whole point of unconditional, no conditions, no point system, no way to earn it. We have to make the daily (more accurately, hourly) decision to live out of the worth and love even when we don't exactly feel loveable.

THE JOY:

When we view ourselves as worthy of love, we can more generously offer that same unconditional and pure love to others. When we give love, we bring joy to the world. When we give from abundance rather than lack or obligation, we bring joy.

FRESH START

the nudge to take risks and find adventure

There's a fine line between stupid and spontaneous; I would say I live on that line a lot of the time. Lord have mercy. The stress I put my poor parents through is insane.

On October 17, 2006, when I was twenty-two, I drove across the prairies and moved to a new city—Calgary, Alberta. I had no plan, no job, no friends. I just knew that I was young, single, and able. I only had $300 to my name—$75 of which I used for gas to get out there. My parents helped me unpack and left me there.

I sat on my front porch and watched my parents drive away after we had unloaded all my important belongings. It was so scary not knowing what was next. I had no freaking clue how I was going to do this. But as the tears streamed down and the fear wanted to take over, I chose a new thought! *I can be anybody in the whole world. ANYBODY. I can be anything I want to be.* I stared out to the street and took a deep breath. I am going to be okay, I thought. Maybe even more than okay.

I was in need of a fresh start, and this was it. No one in my new city had judgments of me or knew my past or history of struggling to fit in or find my place. For a while, I had known I needed more than my small town could offer. I needed to stretch and challenge myself. And boy, did I stretch. This was the opportunity to jump off that daunting cliff of being comfortable and spread my wings to truly learn how to fly. I was nudged that night to create a different life for myself.

And here's the honest truth: moving to Calgary was the stupidest and the best decision I have ever made. Stupid because I had no money or plan, but wonderful because I was suddenly forced to grow up and get real about life. Through following this nudge to go out on my own, I became more fully alive as the person God created me to be. For so much of my life, I had hidden in the shadows; I had played stupid and small because I was afraid others couldn't handle all of who I was. But this moment felt different. Sitting on my new front porch, staring out at my new home, I felt a sense of freedom. And so, I went to sleep excited for the first time in a long time.

Maybe you've felt this before too. So often, we get trapped by what others think is best for us and conform to the idea of who others want us to be. We get stuck in a place of complacency. It is so easy to keep doing the same thing because it is so comfortable. We stay with what we know, what feels familiar and good to us. When it comes to life changes, it is so easy to be stuck and defined by the past. We let other peoples' opinions of us rule how we act or what we choose. People expect us to be a certain way, so it is just natural to keep doing things the way we've always done them. But there comes a day when you work up the courage or momentarily lose your mind enough to do something different. When you step out of your comfort zone and decide to go left instead of right, this is where you can begin to grow and stretch. Be aware that this is also when your friends are going to look at you, possibly judge you, and question why the heck you are going left when you have *always* gone right.

But this is what it means to pay attention to the nudges. I truly had to change my mindset to create a solid future. I had to get out of town to gain perspective. When I moved to Calgary, no one really knew me. No one had any preconceived notions about what my life should look like. This made it a whole lot easier to make massive shifts and adjustments to who I wanted to become.

* * *

This fresh start led me to so many different jobs. At first, I was embarrassed by all the job hopping that I did. Ever since I was a little girl, I dreamed of being a CEO, and I didn't always realize the unconventional paths we sometimes have to take to get to where we want to go. But looking back, there were so many lessons in each role that prepared me for where I am today.

My first job out of college was in Winnipeg as the general manager of a fitness club that was part of a large chain of gyms across Canada. I was originally given the position of sales coordinator, but after twenty-five days on the job and a record month of sales, I was promoted to general manager of one of the worst clubs in western Canada. Lucky me. It was so bad that the corporate headquarters had talked about shutting my location down. I worked my butt off to improve things, working evenings and weekends, even sleeping in the tanning beds (not with the lights on of course) to rest my eyes from the long hours. In a few months, I turned the club around and made my way up the rankings for GM. From this experience, I learned how much hard work can pay off. By putting in hours that others won't, you can get recognized.

When I moved to Calgary, I was all about the fresh start for this new me. I decided to try something new. Instead of managing a fitness club and selling memberships, I thought I would sell boats—because that seems practical for a girl in Calgary. I mean, there is so much water in Alberta . . . (There's totally not, but there were lots of rich people getting paid well who all wanted to keep up with the Joneses.) The city was in an oil boom, and it seemed like everyone was in the market to get a wakeboard or a water ski boat. At the time, I didn't even know the difference between a direct drive and V-drive. My learning curve was steep, but I made it work. The owner hired me because of a recommendation, but the manager of the Calgary boat store didn't like me for whatever reason—perhaps because I am a strong female who wasn't afraid to speak her mind. I had my own office and loved the challenge of showing those men that I knew what I was talking about. And the farm girl in me came out when I would drive a truck and trailer and unload a boat all by myself. If you ever need someone to back up a trailer, I am your girl.

While that job was fun when it started, the environment sucked, and I didn't feel welcomed. Showing up to work where your boss can't stand you and treats you differently than every male salesperson is no walk in the park. So, I left. I really tried hard to make it work, but at some point, you have to know when to stand up and not take any more of the BS they dish out. I truly thought this job was where I was meant to be. But I trusted that nudge to walk away, and I never looked back.

When I quit selling boats, I was in between jobs for a bit. I was in the midst of my job search when my mom set me up on what I thought was a date at first, but ended up being something better: a business lunch with someone at Spitz Sunflower seeds (the best sunflower seeds you will ever eat). A week after this non-date business lunch, I was on to the final interview for the market manager role with the Director of Operations and Sales for Canada to approve me to meet the owners of the company. I was asked to drive from Calgary to a farm in Bow Island, Alberta for an in-person interview with the husband and wife who owned the company. I was given a tour of the full facility and then asked to have lunch with them at their kitchen table. This seemed like my kind of company—no big, fancy, corporate, overpriced lunch. Just a bowl of chicken noodle soup and homemade bread.

I wore heels to the interview, but that didn't stop me from climbing ladders and exploring the farm and packaging facility. I think I impressed the owners with my farming knowledge and ability to hold my own around farm equipment, even in heels. I got the job, and let me tell you—it was a crazy sweet gig. I got a fully loaded Chevy Trailblazer and enough sunflower seeds to last me a lifetime. I worked from home, got to set my own hours, and manage my own territory. I finally felt like I was moving in the right direction to become a CEO.

I loved the company, the environment, and the creative freedom that my role there offered. I had been working there for a little less than a year when I got a call from my boss while I was sitting in my car. He said, "We have sold Spitz, and unfortunately, the new owners no longer want to keep the sales team." It wasn't just me; it was myself and eight others from across Canada that overnight no longer had a job. Just like that, my dream job was gone. I had no clue this was coming. None—not even a hint.

I still remember sitting in my car parked on a side road thinking, *I AM SCREWED!* Tears were streaming down my face, and I was pounding the steering wheel so hard I am surprised it didn't break. I was living paycheck to paycheck. This was not the plan. This was not how it was supposed to go. My world felt like it was crashing in around me. It felt like I had just found this job, and I was getting really good at it. *How could this be happening?* I felt like I was turning into that girl who couldn't hold a job. I'd moved out to Calgary with hopes of landing my dream position, climbing my way to the top of a company, and becoming a CEO. And now, I had to find something new again; I had to start all over. I was so discouraged because I felt like I was finally being valued, welcomed, and accepted. I was gaining traction and seeing the results of my hard work. So, trying to find another company and getting to this place again felt near impossible. I was so hung up on the idea that this job was where I was meant to be. And then, after a minute-long phone call, everything was gone.

Maybe you have been in this position before. Everything is going along perfectly and then—BOOM—out of left field, you get thrown a curve ball that wasn't even on your radar. These moments can really suck and leave a good sting! Kind of like getting hit with a baseball to the face—has that ever happened to you? Dang, it hurts. When you think about it, that moment still probably makes you cringe. That is how that phone call felt. I wasn't prepared, had no warning, and was totally taken by surprise. As painful as it is, it is in these moments that we are being stretched, molded, and shaped. My mom calls this character shaping, to which I always fire back, "I think my character is just fine."

This moment made me question my stupidly spontaneous decision to move to a new city; it made me question this "fresh start." Once again, I was back to square one: broke, jobless, and single. But then, in the midst of my self-pity, the refrain that I had repeated to myself a year before came to mind, "Jess, you can be anybody in the whole world. You can make it happen."

Riding the line between stupid and spontaneous is the best place to be if you want to follow those silly, life-changing nudges. Yes, it will probably lead to failure, pain, and crying in a parking lot. (Wow, great pep talk, Jess.) But this stupidly spontaneous residency will also lead you to become the person you were meant to be. By taking risks, living on a prayer, and following recklessly after your dreams, you will have a greater capacity for life, joy, and adventure. Not all of life fits into an excel spreadsheet.

The unknown, the stretching, the unfamiliar is so hard. But I have learned to press into it. I have fallen a lot, but I have also gotten really good at getting back up. Each time stronger than before. I think we just need to press into the change. We need to make the commitment to ourselves that we will keep rising up, continually reminding ourselves that we can be anybody, we can do anything. We were built for hard things.

If you insulate yourself in what is comfortable for you, you'll never be able to feel those life-changing, butterfly-inducing nudges. If you never ride the line between crazy and spontaneous, you might never realize who you can become. Take a risk: ask him out, apply for that job you've been eyeing, write the book you've always dreamed of writing, start that business, build that treehouse, plant a garden, start running and sign up for a 10k. Do something out of your comfort zone. Do something on the fringe of stupid and spontaneous, and I promise, you will grow and so will your capacity for joy.

THE NUDGE:

Sometimes (ok, more than sometimes), we get nudged out of our comfort zone. When we are comfortable, it can be hard for us to hear and discern the nudges pushing us to grow. Whether it is because we are stuck in a routine and on autopilot, because we are stubborn and unwilling to change our ways, or because we are so familiar with busyness that we don't make time or space to listen, comfortable can be a very dangerous place for our faith and growth. More often than not, those nudges out of our comfort zone are where we find healing, growth, and joy.

THE CHOICE:

We have the choice to settle and stay in our comfort zone or step into the unknown. Usually when we step into the unknown, the nudges and whispers will become louder and more easily discernable. And when we stay in what is familiar, we often lose touch with these promptings. Stepping into the unfamiliar is always intimidating which is why we must remember: joy is better than comfort. When that nudge out of your comfort zone comes, choose to follow it.

THE JOY:

When we choose to step out of our comfort zone and follow those nudges, we are taking action and continuing down the path of joy before us; don't stay stagnant, get moving. Though we can't know what lays ahead, we can learn to trust ourselves and the unknown. In further trusting comes deeper joy.

CHANGE OF HEART

the nudge to let go of judgment

God has a sense of humour.

Really, He is quite funny. You might think of Him as a humourless, gray-haired guy in the sky, but I think of Him as a jokester among the ranks of Robin Williams and Steve Martin. His humour, though, usually changes my heart and life in an unbelievable way. Like the day I met Ishan.

I was in between jobs with no clue what was next and no real plan moving forward. This seemed to be a theme in my life at the time. I was embarrassed that a week or two had gone by and I hadn't landed some big, important job. The economy in Calgary was booming, like really booming, so why did I—Jessica Janzen, future CEO and true mover and shaker—not have my dream job yet? I was supposed to be on track to become a CEO! I was freaking out that I didn't have a job yet and was starting to panic. Money didn't grow on trees, and I still had some credit card debt to take care of (and by some, I mean a lot). I had been living way beyond my means.

One evening, a friend from church started asking me to make a list of what I would want to do and not want to do. I quickly responded without a second of hesitation, "I would never want to work with handicapped kids. They disgust me."

Feel free to fully judge me and punch me in the face. I totally deserve it. Like who even says that?! Looking back now I always think, *Why in the world would I say that?* I hadn't gone to school for that; I hadn't even looked into it. It just randomly flopped out of my mouth. I guess I thought I wouldn't know what to do with them or how to help them. I don't know where this comment came from, but it jumped out. And to this day, I feel embarrassed that I said something so awful.

Now, fast forward to a week after this conversation. As we headed to church, my best friend Carrie asked if I would mind helping in Sunday school. I think they were short on volunteers that day. I happily agreed. I'd already been serving in high school and young adult ministry, so I was more than happy to cover for a Sunday with the little kids. I mean I was a dang good babysitter and a super fun person. How hard could it be?

The moment I walked into the classroom, I saw a little boy in the corner of the room who was in a wheelchair. He sat there patiently, longing to keep up with the other kids. They were running circles around him. All the other kids, who were ages five and six, were running around screaming, having fun, and being goofy while waiting for Sunday School to start. And this other boy just sat there, watching them all run around. He was too weak to even be able to push his own wheelchair.

God nudged me, saying, "Go and ask him to play."

I walked over, asked if he wanted to play with the other kids and if it would be okay for me to push him in his wheelchair so he could join in with them. He happily agreed. From that moment on, this little boy had my heart. Call it love at first sight, if you will.

That was the day I met Ishan, a six-year-old boy in a wheelchair. A few times, his head fell over to one side of his shoulder, and he had to ask me politely if I could pick it up, as he didn't even have the strength to move his own head and get it straight again. He was petite for his age and sharper than any other six-year-old I'd ever met. That was the day I sensed God saying, "Let me show you that these kids are not disgusting but capable, smart, talented, and full of purpose." That day, I received a rightfully deserved kick in the butt about my judgment, and I also learned about Ishan's disease, Spinal Muscular Atrophy, also known as SMA.

We played together that Sunday, and I was his personal assistant. I wheeled him around and made sure he could participate with the other kids in all things Sunday School. When church was done, I felt another nudge. I had all this free time since I was in between jobs. So, I decided to ask his parents if they needed some extra help caring for Ishan. The nudge was fierce, so I wheeled Ishan over to his dad to offer my services.

"Hi, my name is Jess, and I am in love with your son. I know this probably sounds really weird and out of left field, but I was wondering if I could help you out. I am in between jobs and would love to help out in any way I can. I have lots of free time. I've done my criminal record check for the church and can happily show that I am not a total creep. I really just want to help."

His dad asked me to wait until his wife came to meet him, and waiting wasn't a problem since I had nowhere to be. Seconds later, Ishan's mom came walking up, pushing a beautiful little girl who was also in a wheelchair. *Wait, what?* I thought. *Not one, but two kids in wheelchairs. How is this possible?* Then I met Ishan's younger sister, Shanaya, who was also diagnosed with SMA. Totally insane. I explained to their mom, Karen, that I would love to help their family while I was between jobs and my schedule was completely free.

Her next question was, "How soon can you start?"

"Tomorrow?" I responded. "I really don't have much going on."

The timing was a total God thing because I soon learned the nanny who'd been helping this family with all the care had just quit. It was the beginning of summer vacation, and Karen needed help—lots of it. When I left the church that day, I completely lost it. I bawled my face off. I wept for how much of a jerk I'd been for saying what I'd said a few days before. I cried because I could hold my head up and move my neck whichever way I wanted and had never been thankful for that before. I wept because I had two legs that worked perfectly, and I'd never really been truly grateful for them. I just took it for granted that I could sit and stand and run and jump and skate and ski and swim and do all the things without thinking about it for a second. I didn't need anyone's help to feed me, or put me on the toilet, pick my nose, or put on my own pants. I was free. And I didn't even know it.

I went home that night and researched Spinal Muscular Atrophy. Here is what I found and understood: It is a rare genetic disease that attacks the muscles. The body is missing some DNA that does not allow the much-needed proteins to reproduce the nerves, and so they just get weaker and weaker and die off. The nerves are then unable to communicate to the muscles. The mind is never affected. Those with this disease rely on their mind rather than their physical abilities. Before this deep dive on Google, I had no real understanding of what it was like to not be able to do the things most kids went about doing.

The next day, I showed up at their house ready to help with an attitude of thanksgiving and joy. I believed with my whole heart this was where God wanted me to be, to bring some joy to this family. The medical bills were piling up, and the to-do list was long. I spent the next three or four weeks helping out until they went on vacation to visit some family. Those weeks were filled with so much learning. But also, lots of joy and laughter. I was happy to be able to take just a little stress off this family and help out until they found permanent help. It wasn't the CEO position I was working towards, but it was an amazing opportunity in the meantime.

One of the challenges I noticed while working with their family was how hard it was to get funding and good care for their children. It seemed almost impossible to get what was needed. I wished I could help more than I already was. Eventually, the family got long-term help, and I got back to looking for my next job.

***

That day in church completely changed my perspective and softened my heart. Seeds of compassion were planted in my heart that day and continued to grow as I nannied for the kids that summer and stayed in touch with Ishan and Shanaya's family long after that. What I didn't know that summer was that one day, years later, I would have a son with SMA and he would change my whole world. God will often point out parts of our hearts that need to be transformed by His love, then He will place people around us or place us in circumstances that will bring His joy, peace, and healing. I can so clearly see now how that day in church, God was softening my heart and preparing me for my future and fight against SMA.

I know I'm not the only one who has said something or thought something (yes, your thoughts count) that they are horrified by and ashamed of. We think we are saints until that one person or topic comes up. When ignorance or prejudice create an aversion or bitterness in us, we are limited in the ways we can grow and experience joy. We have to get curious about why we feel the way we do or think what we think in order to get at the root of the heart blockage. Awareness of the prejudice is the first step, but once you are aware, you can't stop there. It would be like saying you know McDonald's is bad for you while eating a Big Mac.

You have to lean in, research, and learn about other perspectives.

I couldn't just sit with the awareness that I had an aversion to handicapped kids; I had to open my heart and mind, do research, and interact with Ishan to experience a change of heart. Maybe you have an aversion to kale or yoga—you haven't tried it but you think it's not for you. Maybe there's someone you work with who you don't like and you're not sure why; maybe you have bitterness toward the church; maybe you have a distaste for Instagram influencers and their seemingly perfect lives . . . Whatever it is, whenever you become aware of it, don't just sit in it; get curious about it. Research the benefits of kale and yoga, and try both of them with an open mind. Learn more about your coworker and try to find something that you have in common, or maybe get a better understanding of what they are walking through. Go try a new church, meet new people, and look for stories that talk about letting go of bitterness and experiencing freedom. Talk to an Instagram influencer—message them and get to know them—they are people trying to pay bills and build their dream life, just like you. Only follow those that make you feel good and make you want to be better.

When we weed out places of bitterness, prejudice, aversion, and judgment, we have more room for love, joy, peace, and compassion. Letting go of judgment frees up more room in your heart and life for joy. Don't you want to free up more space for a life like that? I sure hope your response is a heck yes!

THE NUDGE:

Is there anything or anyone that you have a strong aversion to or prejudice toward? Dig deeper and try to figure out what experience or influence provoked that aversion. I'm not asking you to do this to make you feel shame. Remember that everyone has gross parts of them that need to get weeded out—but that is not a reason to stay stagnant and complacent. What areas of bitterness and judgment can you start to weed out to create more space for joy in your life?

THE CHOICE:

You have the choice to either sit in your bitterness and judgment or open your heart and mind to bring healing to that area and change your perspective. When we sit in our bitterness and judgment, those things often seep into our words. When we open our hearts and minds to new perspectives, we are often blessed by an unprecedented amount of joy and a greater understanding of people.

THE JOY:

When we surrender the parts of our heart where there is judgment, we experience freedom and joy like never before. Our aversion and bitterness no longer controls us, and we experience a deeper capacity for compassion.

VALUE VILLAGE MEETS

HOLT RENFREW

the nudge to not settle

There are 7.5 plus billion people on this planet. Statistically, shouldn't at least one person be in love with me? These are the kinds of thoughts that I had as a young, single woman, and I *know* I'm not alone.

I dated in high school for a hot second, but it was never anything much. And then finally, the summer between ending high school and my first year in college, Jeff walked into where I worked, Thunder Rapids Amusement and Go Karts (don't be jealous). He was my next-door neighbor on the farm, and I had always thought he was cute. I had not seen him since his sister babysat me and my siblings when I was in like Grade 3.

He popped into Thunder Rapids, and I don't really remember much else other than he was a total hunk, and I fell in love with him hard and fast. His friends were the cool kids from high school, he played hockey, had a job, was fun to be around, and always made me laugh. We dated on and off for about three years. He was totally incredible. I truly thought I was going to marry him; I wanted to marry him. That is what girls in Manitoba do; you meet a guy, and you're a good Christian girl, so you only date for six months to a year before you get married so you can have sex and carry on with your life. I broke those rules. My parents didn't approve, but I was on my own path.

Jeff gave me a promise ring, and I was sure that this was it. But as life would have it, it got rocky again. We sat in his car one night, and he said he couldn't do it anymore. I was tired of this on-again, off-again thing. This time, I knew that if I didn't hold my ground, we would be back here again in another six or so months.

I told him, "If you walk away now, I will never be able to trust you again. I will never get back together with you." I loved him and desperately wanted it to work.

He said he was done, and that was it. I drove off that night back to my house in tears; I was a total mess. The love of my life—at the time—didn't want me and wasn't willing to make it work the way I dreamed he should. About a year later, Jeff called me and told me he made a massive mistake and missed me. I was single at the time, but I knew I couldn't waver on the promise I made to myself. I knew I needed to stick to it.

* * *

Six months later, I met Karl.* He was in Calgary working construction for the summer. He started coming to the church I attended, and a group of us started hanging out. He had never planned on staying, but things started "heating up," I guess you could say. As much as a good church relationship can heat up. Karl left to go back to the east coast, but we kept in touch. Like every day. Long story short, after months of phone calls, he decided that he was going to move back to Calgary permanently so we could make this official. He drove across

---

* Name changed to protect privacy.

the country for days, stopped at my parents' farm, asked for permission to date me, and arrived in Calgary the next day. He was here. Standing on my front porch. The night he showed up, I was so nervous—palms sweating, heart racing. All I could think was that this was it. I was going to marry this guy. I mean, I had to. He just moved all the way across the country for me. I mean, heck, I have to be committed to this. The guy uprooted his whole life.

Yes, that is right, folks. We had barely hung out, and I was thinking of marriage. Remember that line between stupid and spontaneous? At this point, I was a little unbalanced and seemed to have a full foot in stupid land. But I was young; that's what being young is for, making dumb decisions and learning from them.

The doorbell rang, I opened the door and all I could think was, *"Oh shit, what did I get myself into?"* I took one look and knew I had just made the biggest mistake. Instantly, I knew this was wrong. Fear and panic had taken over me. My head spun in a million directions. What I thought would be instant chemistry was instant panic. The feelings that I had hoped would bubble up were not there. All I could focus on was that I was not attracted to him at all.

Had he not washed his hair? Did he smell? Maybe he wasn't so fresh because he had just driven thirteen hours to see me. I don't even remember the rest of the night, nothing more than the questions swirling around in my head like, *Will I fall in love with this guy? Why is his smell bothering me so much?*

I gave it a week. The morning before I left on a two-week business trip to cover my territory managing Spitz sunflower seeds, he showed up at my house with a coffee and my favourite Starbucks scone. He had written a Bible verse on the napkin and the gesture was so sweet and thoughtful. We said goodbye, and I drove off. Cute, right? I should be smitten. Instead, I was so mad. *How did I not like this guy? Girls would die for moments like this to happen.* But instead of

41

head over heels, I was annoyed. Who gets annoyed at their boyfriend who shows up at their house sweetly to bring them their favourite coffee and scone and wish them a safe trip at 7:00 a.m.? Who gets annoyed at their boyfriend who sold everything, quit his job, drove across Canada to be with them? Karl even stopped at the farm to meet my parents before coming to Calgary.

I should have definitely flown out to where he lived to meet him first and spend the weekend together. I know I just got so caught up because he was the first Christian guy that was pursuing me. So, naturally, I just thought I was supposed to marry him.

I didn't know what to do, so I called my dad.

"Dad, I am freaking out! I mean freaking out. I don't like this guy at all, I mean not one bit. He smells bad, I don't even think he showers. I am not attracted to him at all. Dad, he seriously smells. I can't do this."

On the other end of the phone, all I could hear was my dad laughing.

"Dad, why are you laughing? Why did you not send him home when you met him?"

My dad just laughed some more.

"Dad, this isn't funny. I am in crisis mode. I can't stand him; I don't want to spend time with him, and I am thinking of ways to avoid him. Dad, did you know when you met him?"

"Yes Jess, I knew he wasn't right for you, but you needed to figure that out on your own."

"Well Dad, you seriously could have saved me a lot of problems had you turned him back east."

"You'll figure it out, you always do." I swear this is my dad's most used line next to "it is what it is."

I continued on my two-week business trip. I think sometime on the trip I called Karl and told him I was done and didn't think it would work. I told him we were on totally separate paths and directions. And we very much were. I think I broke the poor guy's heart, but I knew it just wasn't right. Sometimes, you gotta just trust your gut and do the hard thing. Can you believe that I just broke up with the guy over the phone? I chickened out and did it while I was away because I thought it would be easier and didn't have to do it to his face. Kind of cowardly, but I just couldn't bear to disappoint him and see the hurt in his eyes.

Truth be told, I think he knew it would never really work between us. We were just so different. He was so laid back and relaxed, and I was ready to go, still wanting to climb this CEO ladder and have all the nice, fancy things. You know, like owning a vacation property and take luxury trips where we would do spa days and sip wine together. We just had such different visions for our lives. He was go with the flow, and I was trying to make waves. Nothing is wrong with either; they are just different.

About six months later, I was taking a walk with my friend and business mentor Roger. We were out in Banff for a leadership retreat. It was a cold, crisp, snowy night. We chatted about every topic. He chuckled when Karl came up in our conversation. Roger said this and it has stuck with me for life. "Jessica, that chapter of your life will be titled Value Village meets Holt Renfrew. Just two brands that aren't really meant to mix. Two brands with different visions."

That night, Roger seemed to know I was struggling or wrestling with finding my footing again. I had been so frustrated that things didn't seem to want to work out. He encouraged me to just keep going. But most importantly, he encouraged me to be all of Jessica and not let anyone steer me in any other direction. He told me not to worry about what others thought and that great things were ahead. That night sticks with me to this day. Sometimes, we all just need some encouragement to keep going, be fully ourselves, and trust the process.

You might wonder why I've gone to such great lengths to include this chapter of my life that you probably could have skipped over, but I really believe there is someone that needs to read this. Karl is an incredible guy; he is selfless and has a heart of gold and a passion for ministry. But truth is, we just didn't jive, and that is okay. Our visions were in completely opposite directions. And the smell thing, well, there is actual science behind that: some people we are naturally attracted to, and some we are repelled by.

What I learned through these seasons with these guys was that just because something seems right on paper—just because someone gives you a promise ring or writes a Bible verse on a napkin—doesn't mean you're right for each other. And you can't force yourself to feel a certain way. Through these seasons, I learned to trust my intuition; I learned to love myself and the path I was on. I knew that when the right guy came along, I wouldn't have to shrink or change to be with him. During these young, single years, I thought back to that moment with my grandparents—and I knew I needed to hold out for that love.

There is great joy to be found when you stand up for yourself, when you decide not to shrink your plans and goals because they are possibly too big for someone else and it makes them feel uncomfortable. Your roots grow deeper when you decide, wholeheartedly, that you are worthy of steadfast love, when you decide you aren't going to hide any parts of yourself to please anyone, when you decide not to settle.

In seasons of waiting, especially when it comes to your relationship status, remember to love yourself first and foremost. Don't get distracted by other people's paths. That's how you trip and fall. Be patient with yourself and kind. Protect yourself and your heart, trust yourself, find hope in the waiting. But more importantly, find purpose in the waiting. Find purpose in this chapter of your life. Stay the course and persevere—your time is coming. Afterall, there are 7.5 billion people on this planet.

THE NUDGE

Is there any place in your life where you are settling? Maybe in a relationship, maybe a job, maybe you are not using a gift you have or you are holding back because of fear or judgment of others? Whatever comes to mind—yeah, that—that's a nudge, a nudge to change something; so please do yourself a favor and follow it.

THE CHOICE:

Settling in any area of your life is like expecting to go shopping at Holt Renfrew and walking into Value Village instead. You have the choice to either stay and keep shopping, or walk out and go on your way, follow your path (to those swanky designer shoes).

THE JOY

You can find happiness at Value Village; I'm not saying you can't. You can find happiness with a person who doesn't meet your standards, you can find happiness at a job that doesn't excite you and stretch you, you can find happiness even though you aren't using your talent for writing to create, grow, and heal. But joy—the steadfast and unmoving kind—that, my friends, you can only find that joy through loving yourself so much that you simply can't settle because you know you deserve more.

HOT RONNIE

the nudge to go for more

I found out the hard way that selling mac and cheese is not my passion.

When I finished caring for Ishan and Shanaya, it was back to the drawing board to find a job where I could climb the corporate ladder and become a CEO. I believed I had great leadership skills. I longed to inspire people and cheer them on and lead others to a better life. I had led a team and worked so hard at my first real big-girl job, and I missed that buzz, challenge, and opportunity to create. I loved working, I loved business suits, laptops, rolling briefcases, and solving problems. I loved the challenge of trying to be the best. It was something that I felt like I could control the outcome of every time. And so naturally I just pictured myself at the top being super successful. I wanted the life that I saw in the movies. Not a farmer's daughter who marries another farmer. Way too boring for this farm girl turned city slicker (no offense to the farmers). I needed to shift things up again and keep climbing.

After Spitz was sold to PepsiCo Frito Lay, I interviewed with them, only to find that the sales opening was in Edmonton. I finally felt like I had roots in Calgary and didn't want to leave. I interviewed for the job but ultimately turned it down after the position was offered to me. I had great friends in Calgary, and I was involved in a church—plus, I really wasn't excited about the idea of selling potato chips. I went back to the drawing board.

My best friend at the time got me an interview with her company, Kraft Foods, and I landed the position right away. Instead of selling potato chips, I would be selling mac and cheese (huge upgrade in my book). This job was similar to my Spitz role, but now I was with a massive corporation. Little did I know that the freedom and creative room I had at Spitz would be taken away. What they wanted was a robot to follow a checklist. I was beyond bored and found I was not challenged in any way. I lasted less than six months before I was on the hunt again.

Toward the end of my brief stint at Kraft, one of my mentors from church checked in with me to see how things were going. I said I was bored and not that happy at Kraft. He mentioned a company he knew of that had this incredible role that I would be great for.

"Get your resume in shape, and I will get you an interview. I need it by Sunday night."

The weekend I was supposed to get my resume together was spent in the hospital, puking my brains out in extreme pain. It felt like a flu but much worse. The drive to the emergency room was nothing short of comical looking back now. My poor roommate Val not only drove me but also held my hair back as I projectile vomited into a bucket. Picture me screaming every profanity while she gripped the steering wheel at ten and two, trying to get to the ER as quickly and safely as possible. I legitimately thought I was dying; the pain was so horrible. We never did find out exactly what was wrong, but after twenty-four hours of no answers, I was sent home to rest in bed with some meds. It was pretty horrible, and on top of the pain and no answers, I missed the deadline to submit my resume for this dream role. I called my mentor on Monday and explained what happened. He said the applications were closed, the company had candidates lined up, and the role would most likely be filled in the next day or two. Rather than fighting for the job, I just let it go. I decided it wasn't meant to be. I was so disappointed and carried on checking off boxes for cookies, crackers, and more mac and cheese.

A month later, my mentor called me back.

"Jess, get me your resume. Another role at this company has come up. You have to apply for it. Also, they have an employee there nicknamed Hot Ronnie. It could be fun!" He was totally teasing me, as he knew how long I had been single for—almost four years at that point. Yes ladies, four years of being single. I dated some friend's cousin for a hot second, but after date three, he realized I was not for him and got back together with his ex-girlfriend. So yes, maybe you could say I was slightly excited about the possibility of this "Hot Ronnie." I have a hunch that my mentor used this "hot guy" approach to ensure I would get my resume in on time. He must be really hot for another dude to be calling him that. The next day, I worked on my resume and sent it off. A week later, I was scheduled for an interview.

* * *

I remember my interview like it was yesterday. I wore a white, safari-esque coat from Banana Republic, which to this day I still have hanging in my closet. I can't bear to get rid of it because of how my now husband tells me the story about what he remembers from my interview—he remembers the white safari coat.

I walked into the Jugo Juice head office and almost froze. I was so nervous I forgot the name of the guy interviewing me. Totally blank. No name, no recollection of who I should be asking for, just BLANK. I totally forgot to review the details because I was so concerned about looking good. Lord have mercy.

I recovered quickly since I normally do pretty well when I am put on the spot and said, "Jessica Janzen here for my 10:30 interview." I was seated quickly into a board room and brought a tall glass of water. The interview lasted about an hour and a half. As I was leaving, I remember seeing a picture of this "Hot Ronnie" on the wall. They had pictures of each team member on the wall holding their fav smoothie. He was hot—like really hot—he had a twinkle in his eye and a smile that would melt you. I was intrigued for sure, but knew he was probably a total a-hole. *Aren't all hot guys jerks anyway? Now did the interviewer say that Ronnie was leaving or it was Rex leaving? Shoot, I hope it is Rex because Ronnie is hot, and well, Rex just doesn't look like my type, kind of nerdy and way too old.*

I was offered the job, and I had a start date of May 11. I had been in Calgary almost three years, and I was praying that this would be a company I could be at for a very long time. I really wanted to find my rhythm and groove in my career. I wanted to climb the ladder and become CEO of a company. I had dreamed about airports, business travel, meeting my future husband in a hotel lobby over drinks, falling madly in love, and having a whirlwind romance.

Ope, back to reality.

In my first week at Jugo Juice as the District Manager for Alberta, I was expected to create my own magic and drive sales in my territory . . . but things at Jugo Juice were a mess, in my opinion. No systems in place or structure, just mass chaos. It seemed like there was no cohesiveness across the stores. But despite the chaos, I really liked my work environment. Jugo Juice had a small office in Calgary, was locally run, and had a super great family vibe about it. Almost like Spitz did. The office was colorful and filled with pictures of fruit from around the world, as well as photographs of the team members. Walls were painted bright orange. And it turned out, it was Rex who was leaving and Hot Ronnie was who I would be working with. I later found out it was his uncle that owned the company, and Hot Ronnie had been there basically since day one. We shared Alberta as a territory. Hot Ronnie would be responsible for a large part of my training, thus requiring us to spend a decent amount of time together. And I was maybe a little more than okay with that.

The designated trainer took us through the material with the help of Hot Ronnie. He had been at the company for about nine years at this point, so he knew the stores inside and out. A few days into training, it was role play time for customer service. The training facility was a full Jugo Juice store inside of the offices, equipped with everything you needed. That day, I started flirting with Hot Ronnie during the training exercise. Don't ask me why, but I started off the role-playing conversation telling him how nice his eyes were. To this day, I still get butterflies thinking about that moment—thinking about how nice his eyes were and how they had this twinkle in them.

The following week, Hot Ronnie was to train me in my own territory and show me around my stores. I had stores to transfer and sales numbers to fix. And so off we went and toured. We started in downtown Calgary. I felt like I had made the big leagues. I was strutting my stuff around downtown in my heels and rolling briefcase, as business travelers do. Hot Ronnie thought I looked like an idiot and even commented about how big my rolling briefcase was.

During this territory tour, Hot Ronnie and I started to get to know each other. As soon as he asked if I had a boyfriend, I unleashed on him about how all Calgary men were stuck-up know-it-alls and how I was shocked I didn't have a boyfriend. I mean, I thought I was a catch. He didn't say much, but I know he had a lot going through his head, like maybe if I didn't hate all men, I might actually land one.

We stopped at our first store, and Hot Ronnie's girlfriend was there. I got the glare down from her and had no idea why. At the time, I didn't even know she was his girlfriend. He didn't act like she was his girlfriend. It was weird and awkward. Later I found out that just the day before, Hot Ronnie had told his girlfriend that he needed to move back to his parents to pay off debt and get his life sorted, and she would have to move out and find a place of her own. She clearly saw me as a threat. Hot Ronnie also didn't introduce me to her that day, which was mega weird. Anyway, we did our work thing and continued the tour. I didn't particularly like working with Ronnie; he thought he knew everything and that any change was bad. Our management styles were complete opposites. He is patient, laid back, and fun. I am strict and a rule follower. (My nickname was JJ HAMMER, for goodness sake. I was given that name when I was hired to clear up the messy fitness club and literally had to fire almost all of the staff!)

We spent our first business trip out of town the next month in Edmonton. The store opening was insane. The new location was opening in one of the biggest malls in Canada during the busiest time of year—summer break. The store attracted thousands of people daily, and we had no idea what we were in for. Ronnie and I argued a lot about how to set up things. He wasn't open to my ideas because he had done about a million more openings than I had and was set in his ways. I would stay late at the store working and he would bugger off and head back to the hotel where his girlfriend was waiting for him. I mean, who brings their girlfriend on a work trip? How unprofessional!

A few weeks later, we had to open yet another store. It was supposed to be one of the largest openings in the history of the company. A new mall was being built just north of Calgary called Cross Iron Mills and scheduled to open August 11, 2009. I was in charge of it, and I was in over my head at this point. To make matters worse, I had terrible food poisoning the weekend before opening. It was a nightmare; I was green in the face, weak, and feeling like garbage. But there was no calling in sick, so I remained determined to make sure this opening was not a miss. My dad always taught me to stick with it until the job is complete. And so, I did.

I called Hot Ronnie that weekend for help, but he was away for the long weekend with his girlfriend or something like that. I was pissed that he was away for the long weekend, and I was stuck working, even when sick. I did my best to show up. A few days before the opening, I realized I couldn't do the opening without additional help. I called and asked my boss for help. It was so humbling because I didn't want to look like a failure, but knew I needed a team and support to pull this one off. Hot Ronnie was forced to work with me again. This time, the store was mine, and I had more openings under my belt, so I thought I could call the shots. On the day that we opened, Hot Ronnie and I did not move from our positions on smoothie and juice bar for twelve hours. It was so insane that we didn't even stop to pee. At one point, a security guard brought me food because he knew that I had not moved for seven hours straight. But we were so busy, I couldn't even stop to eat it. Ronnie prepped the smoothies with portion packs and juice, and I worked blender bar and passed the finished drinks off to customers. Finally, at the end of the night, security had to shut us down and forced us to turn people away. We probably could have gone till midnight if they let us.

I don't remember much about that day—it was all a blur—but I do remember that throughout the day Hot Ronnie looked at me with those blue eyes and made my heart totally melt. He smiled at me with a smile that would light up a thousand rooms. When I picture this moment, it is as if time stands totally still. It is captured perfectly in my head and heart. In that moment, Hot Ronnie didn't seem like an a-hole. He was hardworking and kind. For the first time, instead of being against each other, we felt like a team. Maybe just maybe he wasn't like every other Calgary douchebag . . .

I was covered head to toe in juice and fruit, sticky and sweaty. We plugged away until the last counter was wiped, and everything was restocked for another crazy day. We set a company record that day, and it felt damn good to work so hard and see it all come together. There is no way I could have made it through that opening without Ronnie. We worked at the mall a week straight before either of us took a break. The mall was the busiest thing we had ever seen, and daily, cars lined the highway to get into see this mega mall. All of Hot Ronnie's family came to visit, including his grandma (who one day asked *me* if it would be okay if she took her grandson for lunch). I thought it was nice that she would ask, but now looking back at the moment, I wonder if their whole family was afraid of me. Was I that much of taskmaster? I know I had high expectations, but what had Ronnie told his family about me that made them ask for permission for him to have lunch? Maybe I was living up to my "JJ Hammer" nickname.

* * *

In my first real big girl job, I worked with people twice my age who had kids the same age as me. I had to level up, and level up quick; otherwise, they didn't take me seriously. When I took over that very first fitness club and got promoted within less than thirty days of working at the company, I had to fire half of the team. It was deathly scary, but I did it. I had to find a new kind of strength, a new voice. My boss at the time coined the term JJ Hammer. Because, well, I had to lay down the hammer and make some big moves. It was in stepping up to a role bigger than I was ready for that I learned so many valuable skills.

In this role at Jugo, I didn't know the juice business, but I did know what it took to turn around a business and make it successful. I had learned very quickly that because I was young and blonde, most people didn't take me too seriously or didn't expect much from me. But I was, in fact, more driven, more ambitious, and more focused than most people double my age. Jessica Janzen, CEO, was my north star.

Sometimes, we can be too fearful to find our potential, to stretch our limits, to learn what we are truly capable of. If we're not careful, we can let other people's opinions define us. There are heart nudges that tell us to go for something that feels a little (or a lot) out of reach. I believe that we are all capable of so much more than we think. Imagine if we all took risks to reach our full potential—imagine how much better and brighter the world would be.

Stretching limits is hard, especially as a woman, because you have likely always been told what you are and are not qualified for. You have most likely been put in a box that you did not build. Maybe you didn't even know that living outside that box was possible. When we are young, we think that we can do anything! Not many limits have been put on us, but as we grow up, people start putting more and more limits on us. If we listen to them, we are seriously hindering our potential, growth, and joy. I know it's hard, but step outside of the box, become the equivalent of a JJ Hammer (replace JJ with your initials). Go for more; you were made for more. Start acting like it, but more importantly, start working toward it.

THE NUDGE:

Apply for the job you're "not quite" qualified for, ask the person out who seems out of your league, move to a new city to get the job of your dreams, go back to school, publish the book or the blog, start the side hustle,the podcast or crazy idea that everyone thinks is stupid. Push yourself beyond what you think you're capable of because, odds are, you are capable of more! You just need to be willing to do the work, stay the course, and go after it—no matter what.

THE CHOICE:

We can choose to let our fear of failure, the limits other people have set on us, and our insecurities get in the way of our goals and dreams, or we can choose to take risks and realize what we are truly capable of. It takes time and learning and mistakes, but choosing difficult over safe is so rewarding. Choosing to step out of the box you've been put in brings so much joy.

THE JOY:

When we work hard and persevere in order to achieve our dreams, we become more and more of who we were created to be. There is a purpose and plan for your life; you have gifts and talents that are meant to bring more joy to the world.

THE SPANISH LOVER

the nudge to listen to other people

Once upon a time, a girl met her true love on New Year's Eve in a rainforest. Sounds like a pretty good start to a fairytale, huh? Based on the spoilers riddled throughout the book (sorry, not sorry), you can probably guess that this fairytale ends with a twist.

I had been working really hard at Jugo Juice, and around Christmas time, I decided I needed a break. The office was closing over the holidays, so my little brother and I decided to go surfing in Costa Rica. When Spitz sold to PepsiCo, our parting gift was a trip of choice. I thought, who better to travel with than my little brother? Off we went. We left a few days after Christmas for a trip of a lifetime.

Hot Ronnie and I were both excited for the holidays, seeing as we were both headed off on tropical vacations. We still never hung out outside of work but shared the occasional joke around the office. We were both in a season of life where being tanned was everything, so we made a bet to see who could come back more bronze and beautiful. The flirtation levels were reaching Jim and Pam from season two of *The Office* heights. Before I even left for the trip, I was already looking forward to coming back and showing Ronnie my amazing tan . . . I also am extremely competitive and felt like this was a competition I could win.

My little brother and I didn't plan much for our Central American getaway. We were gone for about two weeks straight, and in typical Jessica fashion, I had the expectations of someone rich and famous on a luxury vacation but did not come prepared with enough money. Heck, I did not have that kind of money back home either. The only thing that we booked was one week at a surf camp. I had visions of me ripping it up on the waves and getting signed to be sponsored by Roxy or Billabong at the end of the one-week surf camp. You can just imagine how this went if you have ever tried surfing before. It is not as easy as they make it look. Honestly, it is comical that I would even think I could come close to Blue Crush or Soul Surfer status like Bethany Hamilton. I mean, if she can surf with one arm, why couldn't I slay the sport with just seven days at surf camp?

We started in the rainforests of La Fortuna on our first few days for adventuring and exploring. We met some amazing girls from New York City and the cutest guide ever on our white-water rafting trip. Either I was sick of being single or totally in vacation mode (maybe both), but I fell hard for the Spanish white-water rafting guide. He was cute and had a way with girls. The guides we met that day invited us out that night to some local party. Since our new NYC friends and my brother and I didn't have plans, we decided to go for it. It was New Year's Eve and the last thing I wanted was to stay in the hotel and be lame.

We partied with the guides until the wee hours of the morning. I went to the natural hot springs with them at 2:00 a.m. Vacation Jessica did not think as clearly as she should have. We left La Fortuna the following day to go to surf camp, but I could not stop thinking about Carlos—the white-water rafting guide. I called him Carlitos. I was falling for him hard. We had exchanged numbers, and he was sending me text messages and emails that made my heart flutter. I'd never experienced anything like this. At this point, I'd been single for almost five years, so your girl was really feeling it.

In the middle of my time at the surf camp, I left my brother, ditched the lessons and the dream of becoming a pro surfer, and took a bus back up to La Fortuna to see if these feelings were real and this guy was legit. Lord, I have no idea what I was thinking—other than the fact that he spoke Spanish and it sounded so sexy and he was so fun to be around. My head was not on straight. I stayed in La Fortuna at his place, and then took the bus back a few days later. I cried when I left, way more than I thought I would. This was possibly my only chance at love, or so I thought. Carlos and I decided to keep in touch. In those few shorts days, he shared with me that he had a son and he shared what his dreams were. We started discussing the possibility of me moving out to Costa Rica to start an adventure company together. (Screw climbing the corporate ladder, I will just start my own company.) Talk about full-on crazy—this all just days after I met him. Maybe it was the air, or too much coffee, or all the rice and beans, or just maybe my head in the clouds . . . but I was smitten. He was smitten. It was real, and I wanted more of it.

I got back to Calgary, and Hot Ronnie had won the tanning competition. I spent too much time in the rainforest with Carlitos. Carlitos and I continued to talk, text, and Skype. Two months later, I was on plane heading back to Costa Rica to visit and make plans for how this would work long term. My parents were pissed, my friends thought I was nuts, it seemed crazy—but I was convinced Carlos was the guy for me. How romantic of a story is it to meet your true soulmate on New Year's Eve and have this incredible connection? He wasn't a Christian, but his *abuela* was very religious, so I was sure we could make it work. (Insert eye roll here.) My second trip was magical. I was transported to a dream world. We ate endless amounts of rice and beans and drank all the coffee one could dream of. I got to go on rafting trips, and he spoiled me like I was a princess. He showed me off proudly, and the locals accepted me. I dreamed more about starting an adventure company in the rainforest. I thought about how we could get married here and wondered what the wedding would be like and how all of my family and friends would fly out for it, assuming my parents stopped being mad at me. I met Carlos in January and this was mid-March. Two and a half months in, and I was already planning our wedding in my head. Looking back, this is nothing short of total insanity.

I flew back to Canada, and Carlos and I started working on his papers for him to come and work in Canada. Costa Rica's seasons were opposite to Canada's rafting season so it would work perfectly. If I had him here in summer and we could head back down to Costa Rica for the winter, Carlos could work year-round in his field. I would find a way to make my work schedule jive or get a job where I could work remotely, or heck just quit and start our adventure company.

Everyone back home was questioning my decision to date Carlos. One of my dearest friends Marie asked, "Do you really have total peace in your heart about this decision?" And without so much as a second of hesitation, I said "Yes, of course." This was what I believed was best for me. I said this to Marie, probably to ease my own conscience, but the truth was there was a pull, a tug, an uncomfortable feeling that I was fighting against. This is what I wanted, I told myself: an intense, spontaneous love story. I mean, I was basically living *The Notebook*, with a few major plot changes. It's crazy that we let Hollywood movies determine our romance expectations.

I had been single for what felt like forever. I was so sick and tired of seeing all of my friends go on dates, bring their partner home to meet family, have a person to travel with all the time, have someone to explore with. I wanted nothing more than to have someone adore me.

Plus, I think from watching enough romantic comedies, I was really longing for "my person." It's funny how if you want something bad enough, you try to force a square peg into a round hole. Yes, I did feel some bit of dissonance between my head and my heart, but I was trying hard to pray and journal myself into this perfect thing I thought I had to be in order to feel peace about this, about Carlos. I was trying to manufacture my own peace, and I wasn't trusting my own gut.

I didn't have total peace about it. I did have a small tug and nudge on my heart. I was not 100-percent at peace and felt God, my parents, and my friends saying: *This is not the plan for you.* But I wanted love so bad. I wanted a partner and the fairytale ending. I was too blind to see that this relationship wasn't God's plan, but a hodgepodge effort of my own desire. I was so desperate to get married and start the next chapter of my life that I ignored every red flag in the book. My parents stopped talking to me and taking my calls. See, this was a huge deal because normally, we talk every single day. They even called Roger, my business mentor, to seek advice from him and see if he could talk some sense into me. I ignored his questions and all of the nudges coming from friends and family. But I was about to feel the cost of ignoring those nudges.

Sometimes the nudges of our hearts are blocked or cloudy because we let infatuation, desire, desperation, and expectations get in the way of what our hearts are really longing for. We let our desire for immediate gratification take us off the path toward our long-term goals. It's so hard to evaluate the effect someone has on your life, your plans, and your dreams—especially when you are in love with that someone and they fulfill a desire of your heart that you've been waiting for.

I tell you all this to say: we all need people around us who will be real with us. People who will tell us that, I don't know, starting an adventure company with a boy you've known for two and half months is a bad idea. We need people who have our best interest in mind, love us in our mess, and want to see us become who we were meant to become.

Sometimes nudges come from the people who know us best, and listening to them could save you a boatload (or a white-water-raft load) of heartache.

THE NUDGE:

In moments where your loved ones are questioning your decisions and your judgments, listen. I'm not saying they are always right, but sometimes—most times—they really are. Sometimes, you will find yourself on the other side, watching someone you love make decisions that you believe will ultimately hurt them. Speak up, tell them, nudge them—but make sure they know that you love them no matter what.

THE CHOICE:

Listen to those speaking into your life with love. They aren't trying to ruin your joy; they want to make sure you are grounded and standing on a solid foundation. You have the choice to listen, ask questions, and press in or ignore, hide, and get defensive.

THE JOY:

Sometimes we mistake happiness and infatuation for true, deep-rooted joy. I was nudged by friends and family to look twice at what I thought was joy. But I completely ignored their nudges because I placed more importance on what I wanted than what was best for me. Joy comes when we are standing firmly on the foundation of love and wisdom.

ARE YOU OK?

the nudge to be kind and reach out

I will never forget the time I told God I would not invite the hot guy to church.

In the midst of dealing with my Costa Rican lover and managing my parents and their extreme doubt, I still had to maintain my job and life in Calgary. And so, I did. I was in a great spot. I wasn't really into partying, I was still pretty involved at the church, and I was working hard to climb my way up the ladder at Jugo Juice. CEO here I come.

Late one Tuesday night, both Ronnie and I were still at the office. I was a workaholic and maybe a bit inefficient as well. It was normal for me to work way longer than typical business hours. I was also probably trying to make a statement that work was my number one priority, and I would do anything to get to the next level.

After a full year of working together, I had never seen Ronnie at the office late. So, when he was strolling back and forth from the copier late on a Tuesday night, I knew something was up. He hadn't been around much, and I could tell something was off. How do you ask the hot guy in your office if everything is alright? Hot Ronnie and I had never interacted much outside the four walls of the office or in a store. We would only ever talk about work and the specific stores in our territory, or share the ocassional joke about how much we loved tanning and who was darker.

Anyway, that particular night I felt a nudge. God said to me, "Ask him if he is okay." I leaned out from my little cove and rolled just slightly towards him and said, "Hey, are you okay? You seem a bit off."

"Not really." He answered and then paused and continued with a story. "A few weeks ago, my girlfriend and I were out for Valentine's Day weekend at my grandparents' cabin, and someone slipped something into our drinks and drugged us at dinner. Just feeling off. Trying to find my footing but really struggling."

In my head, I am thinking, *Holy shit, this never happens to people I know. This is crazy. I thought this was just what was in the movies or those crazy dateline stories.*

"Oh man that sucks." I wanted all the details but tried to play it calm, cool, and collected. Like what else do you say to that?

Then God nudged me again, "Invite him to church." And in the back of my head, I said to God, "I am not asking the hot guy to church. Are you kidding me? That is so embarrassing, and I already know the answer. There is no way the hot guy is going to say yes to coming to church. Plus, I don't want him to think of me as a Bible thumper."

God nudged me harder this time, "ASK HIM!" The voice was loud and clear.

I quickly worked up the nerve. "Um hey, if you want to come to church with me, you're always welcome. I go every Sunday. It really helps me when I feel off."

I had barely finished asking him before he blurted out, "Yeah, I would love to."

Holy shit, the hot guy said yes. People never say yes when you invite them to church. They just smile politely and say, "Thanks yeah, I might take you up on that sometime," and then file that in the "never going to happen" category and avoid you for a solid few months until they think that you forgot that you invited them to church and won't ask them ever again. Trust me, I know . . . I invite people all the time. And no judgment here—church can be a scary place.

I felt another nudge and this one said, "ASK HIM TO THE GOOD FRIDAY SERVICE!" *No way, God. That is like twice in one weekend. It will be a miracle if he even shows up on Sunday.* Louder this time I heard, "JUST ASK HIM!" in a bold, clear voice in my head that I just couldn't deny. And believe me, I wanted to deny it.

"Hey," as casually as I could, I continued, "If you want to come with me on Friday, I am going as well?"

"You go twice in one weekend?"

See God? I knew that was going to happen. Now he thinks I'm a freak, thanks a lot.

I explained, "Uh yeah, it's Easter weekend, kind of like the biggest holiday for us Christians, you know Jesus dies, gets buried in a tomb, and then rises from the dead and gives us forgiveness and unlimited grace. It's pretty major—hence the Good Friday holiday and day off work."

"Oh, I thought holiday was just an extra day off work. I would love to come. What church and what time?"

I could not believe my ears. Hot Ronnie, Mr. Too Cool for School who lives this mystery life, just said he is going to come to church with me. This is way weird. I gave him all the details, and on Good Friday, I got a phone call fifty minutes before the start of service. "Hey Jess I am here, standing at the waterfall."

"Um great, I won't be there for at least another thirty to forty minutes. I'm still getting ready." I was standing in my bathroom, curling my hair and running late, per usual.

Hot Ronnie had never gone to church before other than being forced through school. Church was not his thing; he didn't know anything about it, but he felt he needed it. We attended the Good Friday service in the morning and went for brunch with friends. Who else was at our table but the very friend who had gotten me the job at Jugo almost a year ago, the friend who first told me about Hot Ronnie.

On Easter Sunday, Hot Ronnie gave his life to the Lord. I knew it was not because he wanted to impress, but because he really meant it. In the middle of the service, I had stepped out to go to the bathroom, and then was asked to help someone who felt ill and was waiting for a paramedic. I missed almost the whole service and witnessing Hot Ronnie giving his life to Jesus. I was mad at first but now I see this as such a blessing, because he could claim this moment as his own. And with faith, you need to be able to do that. Not because you think Sally or Susie wants you to but because you want to. Hot Ronnie later told me about that moment, and I was overjoyed.

I wasn't sure why, but I knew there was something more to Hot Ronnie. Without my prompting, he signed up for discipleship classes and did what he could to learn about what it meant to be a man of faith and follow Jesus. I was a bit confused, not going to lie. Typically, if someone happens to show up after you invite them to church, they never return. They usually attend out of obligation. So, it was weird for me that after that Easter Sunday, Hot Ronnie started coming to church with me every weekend.

At the time, I didn't understand how bad stuff was for Hot Ronnie. For a long time, he didn't really share the details of his Valentine's Day weekend celebration. He was just sad a lot and pretty quiet about the whole thing. He had a mystery about him, and I just let it be even though I was dying to know more. I had no idea how badly he was hurting or struggling until he gave me this letter.

*As reference, May 7ᵗʰ was the night I almost committed suicide.
I think that was the turning point. I prayed the entire night and
finally surrendered. I wrote this letter to you on May 10ᵗʰ. My
story could have ended a lot differently if I never made it through
that night. I owe you my life!*

Dear Jessica,

*I know I can't put into words how much you've helped me over
the past few months, but I guess I'll try. I honestly didn't think
I was going to make it through this horrific nightmare I've been
living, but thanks to you, my family, my doctors, the church,
Derek, Graham, and a few others, I finally feel that I might
be okay. You alone have completely given me hope through your
unbelievable caring and that energy that you have which lights
up the room. I can honestly say I can see God living through you
every time I'm around you or see you. It is very inspiring, and
I only hope that one day I can feel what you have. I know that
nobody is perfect, but as far as I'm concerned, you're the closest
thing to it. Because of what you have done for me, you now
have another lifelong friend, and I want you to know I would
do absolutely anything for you. Words can't describe how I've
felt over the past months; I didn't even know it was possible to
feel like this. I guess after so many years in the fast lane with all
the drugs, alcohol, craziness, and everything else that goes with
that lifestyle, your body is bound to crash sooner or later. Well, I
crashed hard. However, I've accepted my mistakes, and thanks
to you, I'm starting to see there is more to life, and because of
that, I'm getting close to forgiving myself and moving on. I'm
actually really excited for my new journey, and I just hope that*

*God is happy with me and forgives me for all the pain I've given
to myself, to Him, and to others. With that said I'm ready to put
all that behind me and learn from people like you. I don't think
I've ever had a female role model so I guess you can be my first
one, haha. I really look up to you and all I want is to follow in
your footsteps with the way you treat people and help people, you
truly are amazing. I thank God almost every night for the angels
He has put down on this Earth, and I truly believe you are one
of them. Thank you so very much for your kindness. I know you
didn't need to help me at all, but you reached out and helped me
in every way imaginable. I really appreciate everything you do,
and I will always keep you close to my heart. I look forward to
our friendship, working together, and most of all, laughing with
you. You're a beautiful person, and I only hope and pray the
best for you.*

Ronnie

Now if that doesn't make you weak in the knees, you're clearly dead
inside. Like how do you not fall in love with that guy? I remember
the day he gave this letter to me. I had never in my life had such a
thoughtful letter written to me, besides from my mom, of course. My
heart skipped a few beats. Want to hear the cutest part of this letter?
He included a gift certificate for Bed Bath & Beyond because he knew
it was one of my favourite stores—for $100. Like who does that? Hot
Ronnie does that. Listening to this nudge to ask him to church was one
of the best things I could have ever done. I am so thankful I took that
bold step, even though it felt uncomfortable.

* * *

Life is going to get uncomfortable, but I swear, that is where our biggest highlights and best memories come from. If I had cared more about looking cool that night in the office, then I would have missed out on a great friendship and an opportunity to encourage someone who really needed it. When we silence the nudges that tell us to be kind to someone, encourage them, or help them in some way, we are missing out on opportunities to bring more joy into the world. And we all know this world really needs more of that.

Encouraging others is weirdly vulnerable. It's easier to "be cool" and pretend like you don't care about anything. Being "cool" and "detached" is no way to live life; it makes you numb and selfish. C.S. Lewis has this quote that I read in *The Four Loves* (ok, maybe I read it on Wikiquote, sue me):

> *To love at all is to be vulnerable. Love anything and your heart will be wrung and possibly broken. If you want to make sure of keeping it intact you must give it to no one, not even an animal. Wrap it carefully round with hobbies and little luxuries; avoid all entanglements. Lock it up safe in the casket or coffin of your selfishness. But in that casket, safe, dark, motionless, airless, it will change. It will not be broken; it will become unbreakable, impenetrable, irredeemable. To love is to be vulnerable.*

When we open our hearts up to others and show them that we care about them through encouragement or acts of kindness, it's like we are holding our fragile hearts in our hands. And that, friends, is scary as hell. They could take our heart, poke it, throw it on the ground, laugh at it. That's a possibility (another great pep talk from Jess). But I believe that people, most people, are good inherently, and they don't want to hurt you or tear you down. I believe people want to be cared for and encouraged and invited to things. I believe people like it when you show enthusiasm in something, even if they don't like that something. Being excited about something you love shows that you are human. This creates opportunity to relate to one another. Being open and not hiding your heart in a coffin takes great courage, but it leads to more joy, love, and growth than you could imagine.

Walking the path of joy means pushing past fears and the desire to control how other people perceive you. It means being kind because you know what? Kind is cool! It means being enthusiastic about things; it means inviting the hot guy to church.

THE NUDGE:

Sometimes we get nudged to do things that seem pointless. Like asking the hot guy to church, or cleaning the breakroom at work, complimenting a stranger's outfit, or making cookies for your neighbor. We (or at least I) often think, "What good is this going to do? The hot guy is going to say 'Thanks, but no,' no one's really going to care if the breakroom is any cleaner, that stranger is going to think it's weird if I tell her she looks cute, my neighbor can make cookies for himself." But these small acts of kindness show that you care about people and show that they are worthy of being cared for; they are seen and they are loved.

THE CHOICE:

We can choose to either follow through on these acts of kindness and be optimistic about the impact they might have, or we can choose to be cynical and think that they won't make a difference. Think of a time when someone showed you a random, small act of kindness. It brightened your day; it brought you hope and joy. That is no small thing.

THE JOY:

Following the nudges to act in kindness truly makes the world a brighter and less scary place. You never really know what is going on in someone's mind and life, and sometimes just communicating that you care about them is all it takes to lift their spirits. From that, they know they are connected to someone.

LEAP OF FAITH

the nudge to be vulnerable

This is the part where I get friend-zoned three times.

We've all been there. Ok, maybe not all of us . . . But whether it's unrequited love, not getting that job that you really wanted, getting friend dumped, or not having your parents approve of your decision, we've all faced disappointment. And disappointment sucks. And sometimes, we can think that it's a reflection of us. Like we aren't enough and that's why things aren't going our way. But here's the deal: any disappointment that comes is not a reflection of your worth. You are enough for the life you are leading. Someone once told me that other people's responses or reactions don't dictate my worth. This is something that I have to remind myself of a lot when things don't go as expected for me. I can't control other people's responses or reactions, and my worth isn't so fragile as to change just because someone responds in a way that I don't want them to. I learned this the hard way, but I'm a much stronger person because of it.

My feelings for Hot Ronnie were growing, and we were becoming closer friends. He let me in on more of his life. It turned out that his story about someone slipping something into his drink at dinner was a bit of BS. The night was way crazier than he let on. In his past, he actually did a lot of cocaine and drank a lot, although you would never know it as he was perfectly fine Monday through Friday. He had attended Alcoholics Anonymous and had tried several times to quit the crazy fast life he lived. That Valentine's Day weekend . . . Ronnie had been on a bender in Invermere, B.C, fueled by cocaine and liquor. After three days of heavy partying, on February 14, 2010, Ronnie overdosed on methamphetamine. He still remembers his heart wanting to stop, he remembers demons coming to take him away, he remembers experiencing hell.

So, right now, even though my feelings were growing, what Hot Ronnie needed from me was just a simple friendship. It is crazy for me to think that he didn't really have staple "boring" friends. His lifestyle was fast and so, so furious. He truly needed a friend who didn't want to party every Friday night and do drugs and drink until the bottle was dry. Partying wasn't my scene, so it was easy to offer a simple friendship with no strings attached. I had this rad group of friends who were simple and fuss-free, so I just made Hot Ronnie join in the fun.

Strike One

On June 11, 2010, exactly five years after I got baptized, Hot Ronnie got baptized at Centre Street Church. I got to be in the tank with him and dunk him alongside one of the pastors. After Ronnie's baptism, we hosted a party for him at a friend's house. His whole family came; we all brought a dish and enjoyed a potluck together. Funny fact is that Hot Ronnie hates, hates, hates and I repeat *hates* potlucks; I didn't know that at the time. We spent the whole night visiting with our friends who hosted the party. My mentor Graham who got me the Jugo Juice job was even there! We visited with him in the living room telling stories and laughing. After seeing Ronnie and me interact, Graham made sure to tell us, "You two would make a pretty incredible and unstoppable team."

Hot Ronnie and I stayed up late chatting, and at about 1:00 a.m., when everything was cleaned up and we were walking to our parked cars, I couldn't hold it in any longer. I had to tell Ronnie how I was feeling. It was bursting inside of me. I was so proud of him; I was so in awe of his discipline and focus to turn his life around. It was a clear night out and we were on a street in Ramsay that overlooks all of downtown Calgary. It was beautiful. The lights were bright, the breeze was warm. It felt like perfect time to confess how I really felt about him.

"Ronnie, I just want you to know that I love you, like really love you." This was the moment. I just knew he was going to say it back; I could feel it. Everything was perfect—the crisp clear night, the twinkle of the downtown skyline. All of it. But instead, he follows up with:

"Thanks, you've been a great friend."

We hugged, got into our cars and went our separate ways. Talk about awkward and embarrassing. And you guys, here is where things get really sticky. While Hot Ronnie and I spent all of our free time together and I was falling for him fast, I still had my Spanish lover Carlitos over in Costa Rica, waiting on his visa so he could be with me. But spending all this time with Hot Ronnie was making me actually fall in love with him. Ronnie and I had never kissed or done anything, but we had such a great time together. Our friendship was easy and there was no pressure between us. I felt like I got to hang out with my best friend every day.

Strike Two

About a month after I confessed my love for him, Hot Ronnie and I went on another work trip together. When I checked in to the hotel, I found out our rooms were beside each other with adjoining doors.

We hung out every night after work. One particular night, we ended up in the hot tub for two or three hours, talking endlessly. We finally got out after we looked like prunes and went back to the room. Ronnie has quite a sweet tooth and ordered us late-night room service: creme brulees, cheesecake (one of my favourites), and chocolate milk. He wore my extra pajama shirt because he had forgotten his and didn't want to sit in my room without wearing a shirt. As things were starting to wind down, Hot Ronnie mentioned how thankful he was that I was in his life and how good a friend I was for him. He said these exact words:

"I just want you to know that you can tell me anything, and I would do anything for you."

And again, that feeling bubbled up inside. I mustered up the courage to confess my feelings for him once more.

"I think I am falling in love with you. Not I think I am, I truly am. You are so fun and I love spending time with you."

It was like a scene out of Hollywood romantic comedy. Both of us sitting on my bed in our jammies, a tray of room service, me with no makeup on, the two of us just talking about our lives and our dreams.

He responded with, "That's so nice, but I don't feel the same way. How can I love you when I look in the mirror and don't really love myself? We are just really good friends and spend a lot of time together."

His words were like a knife to my heart. How could I be so wrong? He grabbed the tray of room service and went to bed in his room and shut the adjoining doors. I was completely deflated and discouraged.

Meanwhile, Carlos was working hard on coming to Canada, and I still didn't have peace about that whole thing. Now, this amazing newly-Christian guy who had become like a best friend to me was right in front of me. But after all the time we have spent together, he just wants to be friends. I thought starting something with Ronnie was truly the answer to ending things with Carlos. I think I was looking for an out or a sign because I was too scared to actually call it off and admit I had been wrong. Surely, if Hot Ronnie loved me, I could have the guts to call it off.

But Hot Ronnie didn't feel the same way about me. And what made matters worse was that when I found out about his drug overdose, I had offered for him to go to my parents' farm as a sort of "healing retreat." I suggested he go out to the farm because I thought he could find healing and peace. Get away from the noise of the city, you know.

So, I'm still "with" my Costa Rican lover, and Ronnie has plans to bunk up at my parents. Dream come freakin' true. I was not looking forward to the next day of work when I'd have to face Ronnie. And yep, you guessed it: it was so awkward. I could barely look at him in the eyes. When I got back up to my room that night, Hot Ronnie returned the t-shirt I lent him. It smelled of him, and it smelled so good. He had drenched it in his cologne, so much so that I could've wrung it out of that thing. But I didn't mind since it smelled like him in the best way possible.

Hot Ronnie called me later that night and said that he was booking his flights to Winnipeg, where my parents' farm was. I was pissed. How did he even think he was allowed to come after he told me we were just friends? I said I thought it was silly for him to still come, but said if he really wanted to, he still could. I blame my mom for this. I told my mom that I didn't want him to come, and she said I should let him. And so, like that, he booked his flights for his trip out to Winnipeg.

Strike Three

A few weeks later, I headed out to Winnipeg. It was a weird place to be. On one hand, I was waiting for Carlos's visa to arrive, and on the other, I was waiting for Hot Ronnie to land in Winnipeg for a weekend with my family and for him to get a change of scenery. It felt a bit like cheating.

Hot Ronnie arrived a few days after I got there. I remember picking him up from the airport and thinking how sexy he was—tall, tanned, and so damn good looking. All the feelings I had for him were still there. He greeted me with his sweet smile and warm heart and blue eyes. I was madly in love with the guy, even though he didn't like me back. Ronnie and I walked to the car, and I drove us back to the farm.

This was major. Hot Ronnie was at the farm meeting my parents. I hadn't ever brought a guy home since moving to Calgary. We had dinner and enjoyed some time relaxing at the farm. The next day, my dad took us all golfing. He had met Hot Ronnie once before in Calgary when I was moving, and they discovered they both enjoyed golfing. I had started taking lessons because I knew it was an important business skill and good to have in your back pocket. Ladies, if you are going into business, do yourself a favor and book some lessons. You can thank me later when you are putting for birdie and impressing all the big boys. Now, what I thought was going to be a casual game of golf turned out to be the most horrific game of my life. During the golf game, I got the scariest call a girl can get:

You know, when your Costa Rican lover calls but you are with your soulmate who you want to be your actual lover. Yeah, everyone knows what I'm talking about. I answer the phone.

"*Guapa*? It's me Carlos. My visa came through, and I can be on a plane tomorrow and will fly to Winnipeg to meet you and meet your parents. Then fly to Calgary with you!" Carlos knew I was in Winnipeg but didn't know Hot Ronnie was there. Instagram wasn't a thing yet—so there was no way for Carlos to know my whereabouts or who I was with. Sometimes I think it would have been easier to let him know I wasn't interested in him anymore by publicly posting a pic with a new boy. Terrible, I know.

We had been waiting for his visa since the beginning of March. We had waited almost six months for it to go through, and of course, he calls the day I am golfing with the man who I want to be my future husband and my father, who is clearly as obsessed and in love with Hot Ronnie as I am. And I am hiding the fact that Hot Ronnie is even on the trip from Carlos. Not my best moment, I tell you.

I somehow convinced Carlos not to fly directly into Winnipeg and to instead fly into Calgary the day after I arrived back from Winnipeg with Hot Ronnie. To this day, I still don't remember how I did that. The guys were waiting for me to tee off, and as I got back into the cart, I had to tell Ronnie what was all going on. I told him that I didn't really want Carlos to come anymore. But Ronnie said he thought it was great Carlos was coming; he freaking encouraged it. He seemed excited for me. When we finished golfing, my heart felt deflated. All I wanted was for the guy right in front of me to tell me had feelings for me, to tell me there was a small chance, even if it was only a teeny tiny one-percent chance. I would take anything at this point. That is all I wanted. Just a slice of hope with Ronnie to call it all off with Carlos. I still wasn't at peace, and that nudge to call it off was growing bigger and bigger every day. I knew him coming to Canada was a really bad idea, but how could I crush this guy's dreams after leading him on for eight months?

That evening, Hot Ronnie and I went for a run. The runs at the farm are pretty boring. You either run east or west. And either way, it is flat with pretty much the same scenery: prairie fields and odd trees. The saying is that you can watch your dog run away for three days. As we were running, we went back and forth like a pinball machine—I would lead, then he would lead. I was pissed off because he kept looking at me with the twinkle in his eye. He smiled at me differently and was just so damn nice. I didn't get it. The chemistry felt so real.

I could not take it a second longer. I was getting actually mad at this point, and finally I shouted at him, "What is your deal?"

All he said was "You're driving me crazy!" and took off in a bold sprint.

Hot Ronnie is six foot two and can do anything athletic—and do it really well—so when he sprinted off, I knew I did not stand a chance. NOT A CHANCE. So, I let him run. The weather was weird that night. Humid like we lived by the ocean, but also stormy. Lightening was starting to take shape, and I knew a good storm would be rolling in soon. The air was thick, just like the tension between us. I kept running until I felt it was time to turn around. We met just at the end of the driveway and walked the long gravel path back. We walked in the door and headed downstairs to stretch. During our stretch we smiled and flirted with each other without saying anything. We both showered up and then hung out upstairs. There was something between us that night. The desire to kiss and touch was undeniable. At the time, my grandfather's old rocking chair was in my room. I remember Hot Ronnie sitting in that rocking chair. As he rocked back and forth, he laid it out honestly for me:

"I have a weird feeling that if you and I were to ever be a thing, the low lows will be low and the high highs will be extremely high." He paused for just a brief second, "and this, Jess, is just the tip of the iceberg."

And like that, he got up and went to bed.

What the hell is that supposed to mean? The low lows will be really bad and this is just the tip of the iceberg? Frustrated, I went to bed in the room across from Ronnie's. This was not how I pictured the night ending. I couldn't fall asleep that night. I was restless. I pictured me bursting into his room and him grabbing me sweetly and kissing me. At like 1:00 or 2:00 in the morning, I knocked softly on the door of his room. His light was still on, so I knew he was still up. I pictured him opening the door and pulling me in by the small of my back and then grabbing my face and kissing me with deep passion and intensity.

"Come in." He didn't move—there was no embrace like I thought. So, I took the next bold step.

"KISS ME." I said, "Just kiss me and tell me there is nothing there. Tell me there are no feelings. I just know that there is something—a spark, a connection, a flame. Kiss me and find out and if there is nothing. No spark, no love, no chemistry. If there is nothing there, I will drop it and never bring it up again."

I waited with baited breath.

This was the moment. I could feel it building again. And then he says this: "I can't, Jess. I just can't, we are friends and nothing more."

And like that, I left the room and cried myself to sleep. It was horrible. The next day, you could cut the tension with a knife. My heart felt heavy under the weight of all my frustration and sadness, and my pride was totally hurt yet again. I thought for sure after meeting my family, being at the farm, and having a weekend together, Ronnie would change his mind. But he didn't. How could I be so wrong about all the passion and chemistry?

We didn't spend the day together. Ronnie went to visit some friends in Winnipeg, and I did my thing. Later, both my parents drove us to the airport. I am pretty sure they commented on how tense things were. At the airport we sat separately, I put in my ear buds and cranked the music. I was doing my best to distract myself so I wouldn't bawl like a baby. How could I be so wrong about my feelings for him and feel so off about Carlos? How did he not feel the same tension? I swear it pulled at both of us. We eventually had to talk as I had promised him a ride home from the airport. As we were waiting for our luggage, I said "Whoever's bag comes out first has to kiss the other person." He casually agreed. I had a 50 percent chance of forcing the guy to kiss me. A second later, my big red suitcase dropped onto the belt. As we walked with suitcases, I pushed him up against the airport wall and started to lean in . . . But I couldn't do it, I didn't have it in me. I knew I wanted to kiss him, but the question remained: did he want to kiss me? And so, without that kiss, we walked in silence to my car to drive back to our respective homes.

We were driving down John Laurie Boulevard in Calgary, and I randomly pulled the car over on the side of the road.

"Get out of the car." I yelled.

"What?!"

"You heard me, get out of the car."

And there on John Laurie Boulevard, I unleashed on the poor guy—yelling over the top of my little Mazda 3.

"Why can't you just love me? Kiss me, do something. I have a guy flying here from Costa Rica—he gets on a plane tomorrow, but if you just tell me that you love me and kiss me, I will call him right now and tell him it's over. I will tell him to not get on that flight. I will tell him to stay in Costa Rica. Just kiss me and see if there is something. You can't deny the feelings. Tell me that you can feel it too."

I waited for what felt like an eternity.

"I just can't, Jess. I don't feel the same way." He got back in the car and shut the door and waited for me, sitting in complete silence just staring forward at the road.

And just like that, it was over. I had to give up on being with Hot Ronnie—we were just destined to be friends. Nothing more. He needed me for a season, and it looked like my time was up. After I had felt so many nudges to pursue him, I felt so robbed of something more between us. We rode in silence the rest of the way home. I dropped him off and didn't say another word.

I was heartbroken and disappointed to say the least. Why was I not enough for him? Why didn't he love me and desperately want to be with me? I had to sit with the fact that I was still in love with him and that nothing was going to happen; it was uncomfortable, and I hated it. I so badly wanted to control the outcome, control his response (as evidenced by the luggage kissing game in the airport . . .). But I can't control people's responses. This is something I have had to repeat to myself a lot throughout the years.

All these instances of being friend-zoned by the person I was in love with taught me that my worth is not dependent on him. My worth isn't dependent on anyone's opinion of me. Our worth is inherent and unshakable. We were created uniquely and specifically for a purpose. I really believe that. And no one—even when they tell you they don't love you, or say that you aren't pretty enough, smart enough, loud enough, quiet enough—can take any of that worth and purpose away from you. Don't give them powerful permission to break you down. You determine your worth and no one else.

Think about who you are in your core—not how you look, what job you have how, how much you make. No one can define this for you. Only you. I, Jessica Janzen, am strong, fearless, and bold. I bring joy and energy and laughter wherever I go. I am a fighter, and I know what I want. I am here to bring joy and light to the world, and no one can stop me. I am all those things even in the face of rejection and failure.

I am proud of myself for being vulnerable and sharing my feelings with Hot Ronnie three times, even though I was rejected each time. Although it was so painful in the moment, I am proud of myself for putting my feelings out there and being honest. Those nudges to be vulnerable made me more confident in my identity, in following my gut, and in knowing my worth—regardless of what other people feel or don't feel about me.

THE NUDGE:

Whenever we know who we are and that nobody can define our worth for us, we can more easily be vulnerable and take leaps of faith in our relationships. Taking a leap of faith sometimes requires more of a push than a nudge. It takes a lot of vulnerability to have honest conversations with people about where our hearts are at. It takes courage to share how we feel about someone. The nudge to be vulnerable is difficult to act on because vulnerability often makes us feel weak and exposed. But in actuality, vulnerability takes great strength. As Brené Brown says in her book Daring Greatly, "Vulnerability sounds like truth and feels like courage. Truth and courage aren't always comfortable, but they're never weakness . . . Vulnerability is the birthplace of love, belonging, joy, courage, empathy, and creativity." You can't know how the person you're sharing with will respond, but you can know that your worth isn't dependent on it, and from there you can take a leap of faith.

THE CHOICE:

Choosing to be vulnerable with someone is a difficult decision. You also have to choose whether you'll place your worth in their reaction or in the core of who you are. When we choose to place our worth in others' reactions, we will speak and act out of fear and insecurity, whereas if we act from a place of security and firm footing, then we will speak and act out of worthiness and peace.

THE JOY:

When we share parts of ourselves with someone and are vulnerable, we open up opportunities for relationships to grow deeper and to be more fully known by people. Being vulnerable and sharing your thoughts, feelings, and life with others is the only way to more fully grasp the expansive and unconditional love that life has to offer.

CRYING IN TRAILERS AND
KISSING ON CARS

the nudge to do the hard thing

The next day at work, Hot Ronnie and I avoided each other like the plague. No polite exchanges, or talks about how great the weather was, or how fun golfing with my parents was, or how Winnipeg is the best spot to vacation in the summer. I finished my workday and got out of there without even a glance at Hot Ronnie. I was too mad, too embarrassed.

That night, I picked up Carlos from the airport. I was nervous as could be. He came through the doors at the international arrivals gate. I was sweating. I was early, which was shocking because that never happens. All I could think about was I wish this wasn't happening and I wish I was with Hot Ronnie. As Carlitos walked through the sliding doors and greeted me with the biggest hug and a kiss, I froze. The long-awaited kiss in this long-distance relationship was happening, and I didn't even embrace it. Rather, I pictured what it would be like to have Hot Ronnie's lips on mine. I left feeling uncomfortable and that I was living a lie. Carlos slept at my house that night. Nothing happened, I made sure of it. I felt like I was cheating on my best friend. I also felt horribly guilty that Carlos had picked up his whole life and moved here just for me, and this was not what I wanted or what I knew was right for me. The peace never came, and there was always a tug and pull that this was wrong. The next day, I drove Carlos out to Golden, British Columbia to start working with an adventure company guiding rafts down the Kicking Horse River.

I unloaded his stuff and left as quickly as I could. The trailer he was going to be staying in really grossed me out. Just another thing affirming that this was not the life I desired for myself. If this is what owning an adventure company was like, I wanted nothing to do with it.

On the drive home, I cried for three hours straight.

I had really gotten myself into a mess, and I didn't know how to fix it. I knew Carlos wasn't right for me, but I was too afraid and ashamed to break up with him. And for what? Hot Ronnie didn't love me, so I would be breaking up for no reason other than it didn't feel right. Have you ever put something off because you were scared? If, like me, your middle name is procrastination, then you know the anxiety that comes with delaying something you know you need to do.

Back at work, I had yet another store opening to worry about— this one was up in Red Deer, a small town about an hour and a half away from Calgary. I set my alarm early so I could be on the road by 7:00 a.m.

At exactly 7:17 a.m., my phone started ringing—I was expecting it to be my parents calling to wish me a happy birthday—but it was, in fact, Hot Ronnie. We had not spoken for about four days.

"Hey! I just wanted to be the first to wish you a happy birthday."

This was a huge deal for Hot Ronnie—he never did early mornings. I learned that from being at the farm. The guy slept in until like 9:00 or 10:00 a.m. minimum. He asked me what my plans were and I told him, "Just making sure the Red Deer store gets open and then probably dinner by myself at The Earls in town." Super lame, but I didn't have the energy for more. Besides, I don't really like my birthday anyways. I always get let down and majorly disappointed.

But this birthday felt different. Yes, it was a Saturday, and I still had to work, but at least Hot Ronnie and I were talking again. It was so cute of him to call so early. It gave me butterflies again. I drove up to the store happy—still mad I had to work, but thankful Hot Ronnie had not forgotten me.

Then in the afternoon, I got yet another call from Hot Ronnie. It was so weird that he was calling twice in one day.

"Hey, so what are your plans again tonight?"

"Working and then dinner by myself. Not much has changed in the last five hours since we spoke."

"Well, I think you should come to my parents' place. We're having this massive garden party for my grandparents fiftieth anniversary and it will be super fun. There is a ton of food, and I would really love if you could come. You shouldn't spend your birthday alone."

"Um, I am not sure if I can swing it. The store has so much work to be done on it."

"Just come. I am sure it will be fine. You can't spend it by yourself."

And so, just like that, I did something I would have never done and left a store opening early. I left Red Deer around 5:00 p.m. to race back to Calgary to shower and change. I rinsed off, curled my hair, touched up my makeup and then threw on a long, striped dress, and headed up to his parents' place.

When I arrived, there was no place to park, so I called Hot Ronnie to help me find a spot. He walked out, found me a spot, grabbed my hand like we were dating, and whisked me to the backyard. Walking into the yard was nothing short of magical. Ronnie's dad was a landscaper, and the party looked like a picture out of a gardening magazine—white tent, beautiful flowers everywhere, and torches and twinkle lights to set the mood.

As we were walking down the path, some of Ronnie's family friends came up the path and said, "Who is this beauty? Is this your girl?"

"She sure is," he responded.

What was happening? My mind couldn't keep up. All I knew was that I wanted to enjoy the night, and so I did. Ronnie had called a few of my friends and also had them show up and surprise me. We ate together and laughed. We had the best night. I didn't know anyone there, most of them were north of sixty-five. I remember standing in his mom's kitchen and saying to her, "I am going to marry your son one day. Just watch."

My friends left after cake, and Ronnie and I stayed talking and laughing. As the really old folks left, the music came on and we danced. The last song of the night was by Tim McGraw and Faith Hill. It was after 1:00 a.m., and we danced right out of the tent into the quiet of the yard. Away from everyone. The chemistry and connection I felt in Winnipeg was back and stronger than ever.

How could this be happening, I thought. This was the moment every girl dreams of.

I was starting to fade, given the fact I had been up since 6:00 a.m. and worked a full day. In the morning, I would have to get back out to Red Deer and be at the store by 8:00 a.m. Every part of me wanted to stay, but I knew I had to get going. Ronnie offered to walk me to my car. We held hands and walked in complete silence. As we got to my car, he pushed me up against the car door and brushed the hair out of my face, and looked straight into my eyes with the twinkle in his. He cupped both hands softly around my face.

"Why do you like me so much, Janzen?"

"Well it's your heart, and how much you love Jesus, and . . ." and without any hesitation, he leaned in and kissed me. The kiss I had been waiting for. It was long and passionate—he pressed his body closer to mine, and I could feel my knees weaken and heart racing. It was the most romantic thing that had ever happened. I had been waiting for a moment like this my whole life. It was a scene out of a Nicholas Sparks movie. So heated and filled with fire. When the kiss finally ended, he opened my door and sent me on my way.

It was well after 2:00 a.m., and I couldn't contain my excitement. I even called my mom to tell her. She was so confused, as it was the middle of the night . . . I apologized and told her to call me when she got up.

I worked the next day, and all I could do was replay the memory of him kissing me over and over again. I didn't care that I was working yet another weekend. My life was complete. I could die, because as far as romance goes, I had achieved it—Hot Ronnie kissed me on my birthday. It was the best birthday present a girl could ask for.

The next few weeks, we exchanged winks and glances at the office and kept things under major wraps for a long time. We worked a golf tournament the following week, and he asked me to join his family for dinner one night. He was still living at home paying off debt, and staying 100-percent sober. He knew I was trying hard to eat healthy and was on this big Granny Smith apple kick, and so he stopped at the store to pick up apples for me and brought them out to the golf course. He listened really well and made note of the important facts. I still smile thinking of the Granny Smiths he brought me.

* * *

Remember Carlos? Oh, you forgot about him for a second? Me too.

In the back of my head, I still had to take care of unfinished business. Mid-September, Carlos finally had a ride back to Calgary with some of his co-workers and decided it was time for us to spend the weekend together. I was dreading this. Carlos and his friend stayed at my apartment. I told him it was too crowded for me so I would stay at my bestie's place that night since it was literally just blocks away. Never in a million years would I have thought about hiding my journal that was beside my bed. It was buried in a stack of books, but Carlos found it that night and read through it all.

He read about my feelings for Hot Ronnie, he read about me feeling stuck with him and how I had to break it off, and he read about my magical kiss with Hot Ronnie. The next morning when I arrived at my apartment, I could feel that things were not good before I walked into the room. He was crying and so upset. I don't remember the details, but I took him for a nice steak dinner and told him it was over. I guess I felt an expensive meal would help me feel less guilty. I was honest with him and told him that the biggest reason was that Hot Ronnie went to church and loved Jesus. I knew I needed that in a partner. Carlos offered to come to church and change— he begged me—but I knew it would not be for the right reasons.

And so just like that, my Spanish lover was set free, and I was fully focused on Hot Ronnie.

I wish I had done the hard thing sooner and broken up with Carlos. But I didn't. And I learned from it. Through all this, I learned to trust my gut and speak my mind more. I learned that putting off something out of fear takes away from the joys in life.

THE NUDGE:

Have you ever been too stubborn to end something because of fear and shame associated with it? Trust me, it will get much worse if you don't trust those nudges and tugs on your heart. Don't wait—do the hard thing.

THE CHOICE:

If you know what your heart wants, don't settle. Choose to go after what/who you truly want and don't settle out of desperation, timing, and a plan that you thought should go a certain way but is looking completely different.

THE JOY:

Though you may have to wait and work for it (and confess your love three times), it always brings more joy to follow the desires of your heart than to settle for less.

FALLING IN LOVE
AND FALLING APART

the nudge to be the hero of your own story

This is where the fairytale ending happens . . . except, oh wait, we're only halfway through the book. Just stick with the story—trust me.

Yep, Hot Ronnie was finally my boyfriend! This was everything I wanted. But things were weird. I was more into him than he was into me. I felt like sometimes he dated me because he felt like he owed me for being a good friend. It was really hard to have such intense feelings for someone and not have them totally reciprocated.

Usually, the first year or two of any relationship is pretty easy, you are totally in the honeymoon phase and just enjoy each other. You take off on whirlwind trips, you go on double dates with all your friends, you soak up being carefree. You haven't moved in, you sneak in sleepovers, your bank accounts aren't merged yet; it is simple. Well, that was not at all how it looked for us. It was messy, full of expectations from me, full of confusion for him, brimming with challenges, and so much more.

I felt like our relationship should always have the same intensity of our first kiss on my car. Boy, was I wrong. It wasn't even close. Ronnie never introduced me to his friends; if we bumped into someone he knew, he would forget I was even standing next to him. I felt like a lost puppy patiently wagging her tail. We did stuff together, but I never felt fully included. Almost hidden, in a sense. It was like Ronnie was stuck between two completely different lives. He was lost.

After we started dating, Ronnie told me more about his past. I learned that Ronnie had been using drugs since he was about eighteen. We're not talking about just smoking weed occasionally. He did hard drugs. Stuff I had never seen. Around the time he had that overdose on Valentine's Day, he was trying to clean up his act. But he hung out with the wrong crowd and overdosed on meth.

He should be dead, or at least brain dead. One of the guys slipped in 1500mg of meth into his cocktail. It's enough to kill you in a heartbeat, but somehow, by God's grace, the drugs didn't kill Ronnie. Ronnie just remembers going completely gray, reaching for a phone to call 911, and never being able to place that call. Swinging his arms uncontrollably, almost seizure-like, and passing out. He remembers demons waiting to take him, lying there hopelessly. By God's grace, the next morning he woke up, grabbed a piece of paper, and started writing a letter. Begging God for one more chance. He had never written a prayer before, but was in such darkness he felt that was all he could do to possibly survive.

Ronnie has not touched drugs since that night. It has been ten years. And he won't ever. His recovery was crazy; instead of illegal drugs, he was put on every prescription possible. These medications had weird side effects that affected his mood, but I let it slide. I never knew how much medicine he was on or exactly what he was taking. He never made a big deal about it. Truthfully, I never saw him take them. He just silently did his thing. While he was battling depression, unbearable anxiety, and severe insomnia, he was also trying to find new footing because he had totally transformed his life after his overdose. Imagine starting life over again at the age of twenty-six . . . it was not easy.

One day, Hot Ronnie had finally hit his wall of all the drugs his doctor had put him on. He was on every anxiety, anti-depression, and sleeping pill you could imagine. When I've asked him about it, he recalls being completely numb for the first two years of our dating relationship. But one night, he decided he wanted to taste food again and be able to process and truly experience life instead of numbing it out.

The day he decided to get off all his meds, I couldn't get a hold of him for a while. He had been gone, and I had been calling and texting him. He finally answered and asked me to come over. When I got there, he was in a cold sweat. He was shaking violently, and it looked like a scene from one of those TLC rehab shows.

"What's wrong?" I asked.

"I cut myself off all my meds and am struggling—like really bad. I think I need my parents or food or I don't even know. I feel hopeless. This is harder than getting off the cocaine." He mumbled as he continued to shake and sweat.

Without hesitation, I ordered my favourite Indian food and got him in my car. We picked up the food and headed to his parents. We sat in their front living room, and he bawled. He was scared and worried. The next day, I booked him into see my naturopath. I wanted so badly to heal him and make him better. She has fixed so many of my health issues, and I knew she could help him. She gave Hot Ronnie clarity on what his body was missing and how he could supply it with nutrients and vitamins so that he wouldn't have those crazy dips again. To this day, he is still crazy obsessive about his vitamins. We have three shelves full, and I am beyond proud of his work to continue to stay healthy and stay off those meds. Please note, I am not a medical expert and I believe there is a time and a place for medication. Always consult your doctor for what is best for you.

* * *

After we had been dating for a year and a half, which is, in my book, like the perfect time to get engaged, I thought *for sure* Ronnie would pop the question. But instead of asking me to marry him, he asked me to move in. I was so pumped; I spent all my time at his place anyway. And so, I gave my notice at my apartment and moved in.

I knew it was "wrong" for a Christian girl who goes to church to live with her boyfriend before getting married, so I didn't really talk about it that much. I didn't even tell my parents because I knew they would be so disappointed. But I knew that a proposal was coming—it just had to be soon.

It was a bit intense working and living together, but we managed. Hot Ronnie had taken up a second job in the evenings to help continue to pay off debt at a bar called Flames Central. Not the greatest spot for a guy who was previously an alcoholic and struggled with drug use, but the money was good and the job was easy.

Then one night in March, Hot Ronnie wasn't answering my calls or text messages before bed. I couldn't wait up any longer and fell asleep. I had a weird feeling in my stomach but trusted that he was fine. At about 4:00 a.m., Hot Ronnie walked in and stunk of booze, actually reeked of it. I was furious.

"What the hell," I yelled as I sprung out of bed, "I thought you said when you were going to start drinking again, it would be with me and super special." I pictured a fancy restaurant downtown with an expensive bottle of wine. Hot Ronnie had just gone over 800 days of being totally sober. Had not touched a drop. And just like that, it was done and over. I could tell he hadn't just had one drink but several. I could smell his breath from across the room. I have never been that mad at someone in my life. I was angry at him for being dishonest, for not including me, for jumping off the deep end after working so hard to get his life on track. He said sorry, explained that it just felt right, that it was totally innocent, and that he wouldn't do it again. He shrugged it off like it truly wasn't that big of a deal. I was beyond hurt.

A few days later the exact same thing happened. He went MIA. I could not get a hold of him, and when he eventually got home, it was some ungodly hour. He stunk of booze again.

I nagged and yelled and cried, and nagged some more.

And two days later, he came home from work and said, "Here are the keys to my truck, I want you out by the end of the night. I can't do it anymore." It hadn't even been two months since I moved in.

He grabbed my car keys and left.

I fell to the floor and sobbed and sobbed and sobbed. I even blew my nose in the bed skirt. I was so mad that I thought at least leaving him my gross boogers would be some sort of revenge. Plus, I couldn't pick myself up off the floor to get tissues. How was this happening? The man of my dreams was over it. I called my bestie Jenn and her little sister, and they were over within five minutes of the call. We packed up all my clothes and important items, and I left, just like that. Ronnie and I switched vehicles the next day at work. He didn't even look one bit sorry. I knew he didn't want to talk about it or discuss how we could make this work. There was no emotion, no apology—just over it. I called my mom, and she was on the first flight out the next morning. I was a mess. She got a hotel room, and we had a slumber party for a few days. I cried and told her everything. There was never a moment of judgment. Just pure, unconditional love.

Those were some tough months. Ronnie continued to drink and started dating every girl in Calgary, and it would show up on social media. He would come into the office some days still smelling of booze. It was horrible. I was heartbroken. All of that hard work and church time together, and it felt like everything was just thrown out the door. Ronnie was acting like the last year and a half had meant nothing, like it never happened. The hole in my heart and pit in my stomach were ginormous.

Last chapter, you were probably thinking Hot Ronnie went to Rom-Com University and graduated top of his class. He was the nice, hot, good-smelling Christian boy I'd been waiting for. He was going to treat me right and love me well. But no. Hot Ronnie was not, in fact, perfect. He was not my knight in shining armor, he was not the prince in my fairytale, not the hero who saves the damsel in distress. I had all these expectations of him, but in that year and a half of dating, he didn't really treat me well. He didn't love me the way I craved to be loved. I felt like I had to earn his love, and I was always coming up short. He was never bad to me, but I always felt like I was putting way more into our relationship than he was.

While I'm not excusing how he treated me, I also know that my expectations of him were unrealistic. I have crazy high expectations, and that can be a great asset in business but a massive road block and hurdle in a personal relationship. Ronnie was going through a really tough season and trying to sort through stuff that I couldn't really understand. There's a difference between having high standards and having high expectations. I never recommend lowering your standards, but sometimes I think we all need to lower our expectations or get rid of them all together. Standards are about the character and quality of a person, seeing and knowing who they are at the core. Expectations are about the things you want from the person. For example, expecting every day of dating to feel like our first kiss on my birthday after the perfect party in the garden in his parents' backyard—that's an expectation (an unrealistic and dangerous one). Knowing that I wanted to date a Christian—that's a standard and one that shouldn't be lowered. Having unrealistically high expectations doesn't account for the other person's humanity: they aren't perfect, they can't read your mind, they can't always make you feel a certain way. My expectations of Hot Ronnie were unreasonably high and put too much pressure on him. In the end, it was these unfulfilled expectations that left me more heartbroken.

Evaluate your expectations in relationships. Are they reasonable or unreasonable? Try writing some of your unspoken expectations down: *I just want him to know when I'm sad and say something really nice and heartfelt. I just want him to make me feel like I'm the only girl in the world. I just want him to heal my insecurities by identifying them and then encouraging me in those areas without me having to map everything out for him.* Any of those strike a chord? Anyone? Bueller? You there? Some expectations might be healthier and more realistic: *I want him to introduce me to his friends whenever he runs into them. I want him to talk with me about his struggles—even if I can't fully understand, I can support and encourage him.* As you make your own list, try to determine which expectations help to build a healthy relationship and which ones don't. You can also do this with friendships, your parents, or your boss. When we don't verbally identify our expectations, we can often feel unsatisfied but not know exactly why. And having loads of unrealistic expectations can leave you heartbroken, like I was. Miserable. Pitiful. Pathetic.

Finally, one day during my weekly one-on-one with my boss Kara, she got through to me. She had noticed I was doing terrible and paused everything. She stopped caring about work and the results and the to-do list and dove into my heart and the hurt I was feeling. She told me, "Jess, this will be the biggest mistake of his life. He has never had better and will never find better, but you can't keep letting him win. Move on with your life and get going. This is his mistake, not yours."

I love that. This is his mistake, not yours. So often, we get so upset

101

with ourselves when something in life goes a different way than we thought it should. We get mad at ourselves for making a mistake and we end up staying still and stuck. We don't allow ourselves to move forward. I didn't want to stay stuck or let him define where I was any more. This is where my habits really started to develop.

I took Kara's advice. I got going in ways I never knew were possible. I signed up for my first half marathon. I committed to becoming a spin instructor and got into the best shape of my life. I would often work out at the same time Ronnie would work out so that I could run into him. Eventually, I was emotionally strong enough that I didn't have to force myself to run into him to feel ok. I had amazing friends, they lifted me up when I had no strength. I found people who wanted to support me.

Getting moving was the best damn thing for me. I was able to breathe. My heart wasn't over Hot Ronnie, but I had to trust that it would all work out. He wasn't slowing down for a second. He continued to date up a storm. Two could play this game. I went shopping. I got a makeover. I bought colorful, bright pants. I changed my mindset. I worked on me. I started to fall in love with myself again. I got through April, then came May. May turned into June. Still no communication, no remorse, no emotion from Ronnie. He was still out on the town. Coming up on social feeds everywhere. The complete life of the party that he had so desperately tried not to be a part of any more. I was worried about him. I still loved him and cared for him so much. But I was not willing to give in and put up with his choices. It wasn't what I deserved. It wasn't what God wanted for my life. It was like a nudge the other way—to wait, be patient, and let things work themselves out.

Kara's advice to move on and get going really resonated with me. I was grieving my prince, my knight in shining armor, and she snapped me out of it. She woke me up. He was not my hero; he wasn't going to save me or rescue me from the pesky dragon known as singleness. The truth was: I'm the hero. I'm the damsel, but rather than sitting in my misery distressed, I made the choice to be determined. Determined to take my life back, determined to not let this boy define me, determined to keep going down this path of joy I was on. I didn't need a partner to bring the joy; I could bring it myself!

Kara's nudge really empowered me. I got back up, I washed my face (thank you Rachel Hollis), and I started acting like the hero I already knew myself to be. I took care of myself and set reasonable expectations of myself. I was kind and loving and compassionate with myself.

When life knocks us down, which it's bound to do, we can either be passive observers and watch our life go by, or we can be active participants, running down the path of joy. We can ignore the nudge to get up and wash our face, or we can follow it and then keep following the nudges that encourage us to be the heroes of our own stories.

THE NUDGE:

When we are knocked off our feet from circumstances that are beyond our control, we can feel helpless, confused, and like everything is ruined. It's so tempting to hold onto what once was, what used to be, because then you can sit in pity and nostalgia instead of actually doing something. When the nudge comes to get up and shake yourself off, I encourage you to follow it. Rise up my friend. Rise up, and then do it again and again because finding joy is never a one-and-done opportunity. This is life, and I have learned that it is in the rising that we get stronger.

THE CHOICE:

Choosing to stand up after you've been knocked down takes courage and perseverance. Even though you won't feel like carrying on with life most days, it is important to keep getting things done. When we choose to stand up and dust ourselves off, that's when we grow, we expand our capacities, we reach our potential. Getting back up again helps you believe in your own worth, because you are acting out of your worthiness.

THE JOY:

Joy comes when you look back and see how far you've come. When you circle back, you can say, "This is where I got knocked down, but I'm so much stronger now than I was back then." Continue to rise back up. Trust me, it is so worth it.

THE PARKING LOT

*the nudge to live in abundance
and not take scraps*

Wedding time! Don't worry, you didn't miss a page, I'm not talking about my wedding.

When I moved in with Hot Ronnie in January, one of my girlfriends had sent out wedding invitations and invited me and Ronnie. I could not have been more excited since I had never really travelled with a guy (except Carlos in Costa Rica). I had always dreamed of traveling with my boyfriend. Hot Ronnie had become good friends with my friend Val, too, so I was kind of hoping he would still go. I was also praying that he would maybe wise up and get back together with me. One day at work, he was walking by my office to get to his desk, and I asked if he planned on still attending the wedding. He casually responded, "No, I cancelled my flight a long time ago," with zero emotion and walked on.

Every time my phone rang with Hot Ronnie's number on caller ID, I was convinced he was calling to get back together with me. Sadly, it was always work related: had I placed the opening order, were the franchise partners ready and trained, blah, blah, blah. Always work, nothing about us. On Canada Day, I got a call from Hot Ronnie outside of business hours, pretty late at night. Rather than answering, I sent it to voicemail and carried on with my plans. I was still pissed he was missing Val's wedding, pissed he asked me to move out, pissed we broke up. A few days later, I was all packed up and ready to leave for the wedding. I decided to leave my car in the Jugo parking lot and just take a cab from the office to the airport to save some money. The morning I was scheduled to fly out, I drove to work but needed to talk to my mom before starting my day. Things had been weird with Hot Ronnie ever since he called on Canada Day. Even though I didn't answer the phone that night, he had been more flirty. He was walking by my office way more, trying to get my attention for no reason. However, there had still been no dialog, no sorry, no nothing. I was totally heartbroken and confused. It was just after 8:00 a.m., and Hot Ronnie's truck was already in the Jugo parking lot, which was odd for him since he was not an early riser.

I called my mom on her cell—no answer. I called the house line, and my dad picked up.

"Dad, I need to talk to mom. Is she there?"

"She is tied up at the moment."

"Dad, it's an emergency. Get her."

"Sorry, she can't come to the phone, she is on another call."

"Dad, it's serious, I need mom—tell her it is 911."

"Well, is there something that I can help you with?"

"No Dad! This is a Mom thing. Ronnie is driving me crazy and being a total a-hole and starting to flirt with me again. And I just got strong and stopped caring but it is messing with my head—I NEED MOM."

"Well Jess, I am sure it is all just a misunderstanding, and the two of you just need to have a sit-down conversation where you can both share your side and how you are feeling."

"Dad, he is an a-hole, and I don't want to understand his side. He broke my heart and is starting to flirt with me again, along with every other girl in Calgary—I can see it on social media. It is so confusing and NOT OKAY!"

Wanna hear the crazy part? What I didn't know about that exact moment is that a few cars over, Ronnie was in his truck on the phone with guess who? MY MOM—hence why she was tied up and my dad wouldn't ask her to get off the phone. Hot Ronnie was telling her that he had made the biggest mistake of his life and wanted me back. He told my mother he had noticed some positive changes in me and felt like I was more ready. I didn't understand this at the time, but I do now. He needed to be by himself for a few months to ensure he had confidence in who he was and ensure he was choosing me, not just going along with what felt right. And I guess my dad knew some of their conversation and was trying to talk me off a ledge because he already knew what was coming.

I eventually hung up on my dad and went in to work, still pissed that I had not talked to my mom. I couldn't wait any longer for my mom. I found out this part about Ronnie being on the phone with my mom much later.

I am not sure why, but Hot Ronnie ended up driving me to the airport for my flight. Maybe he felt bad; I didn't really care why. I was going to take the free ride and save some cash. I was secretly hoping that he had a bag hidden and was going to be like "Just kidding! I love you and am coming with you."

No such luck, and I was working on being more realistic. While I was off to the wedding, Ronnie was gearing up for Stampede at home. For those of you who don't know, Stampede is an annual rodeo that happens in Alberta. There are rodeo events, concerts, stage shows, agricultural competitions, and really good food with a midway. It is considered the greatest outdoor show on earth. It is a hoot and a half. It was Ronnie's first Stampede since he had given up drinking, and let me tell you, this guy lives for Stampede. Here I was, hoping for some grand gesture at the airport. (After all, he *had* been flirting with me.) But alas, he dropped me off at the airport and went on his merry way to his first of many Stampede parties. I reminded myself that while yes, Ronnie was flirting with me again, he was also flirting with every other Calgary girl. Miss Realistic was off to Val's wedding, and I was convinced Mr. Stampede was in his element, not really thinking of me at all.

The wedding was beautiful, and I had a blast exploring Victoria. I flew back to Calgary late Sunday afternoon and hopped into a cab to get my car in the Jugo parking lot. As the cab driver pulled into the parking lot of the office, there was Ronnie sitting on the back of his tailgate in all his cowboy getup.

WHAT THE HECK?!

Ronnie asked me to sit on the tailgate and said, "Can you just listen to what I have to say?" He pulled out two pieces of printed computer paper that he had typed on and read me this:

Dear Jessica,

Knowing how long you keep my letters, I'm writing this hoping you'll keep this one for a really long time, longer than all the others. I've made a lot of mistakes in my life but I'll be damned if you're one of them. You're my guardian angel; I've believed that since the day you asked me if I was okay. While I sit here writing this, I try to help myself understand why I tried to convince myself that it was over, and the truth is, it's because I was scared. And I'm still scared. I'm so afraid that I won't be everything you deserve. But if you give me one more chance babe, I will give you all my heart and soul for the rest of your life.

I am so sorry for the pain I have caused you over the past two years, and especially over the past couple months. That was never my intention. Seeing you not yourself around me cuts through my body like a jagged knife, and I can't take it anymore. You're way too precious to me and I care for you way too much. I, too, let my pride get in the way and I'm admitting now that it was wrong and completely unfair to do to you. After you told me you were moving out, I didn't want to be the one that was hurt the most, so instead of running after you like a real man would have done, I pushed you away instead. It was selfish, weak, and incredibly stupid. I know I don't deserve you, I haven't deserved you since day one, but for some reason you've stayed by my side, you've watched me crawl through shit and come out clean on the other side, and now that I'm clean you deserve more of me rather than less just because I made it through. Maybe I did use you a little bit over the past two years, but to tell you the honest truth, I wouldn't have made it through without you. I've been through hell and I haven't enjoyed it at all and maybe that's why it clouds my memory on a lot of our relationship, but that doesn't mean it hasn't meant the world to me. I love our incredibly unique story; I love how you saved me, and how I'm your boy. I always want to be your boy forever and ever.

I let my ego go to my head a bit and that wasn't fair to you. I just felt like I was getting my groove back and feeling that confidence that I used to feel all the time. However, God has humbled me again and has put on my heart the important things in this life, none of which are carrying on until 4:00 in the morning unless you're giving birth . . . I also cannot tell you how sorry I am for not sharing in that first drink with you. To this day I regret that decision and I can't believe how selfish it was. I sometimes have no idea what goes through my crazy head, and I wish I could control it more than I do. I know how much that hurt you and I completely understand how you feel. Again, another selfish move on my part, and I am sorry.

I know I could probably go on without you, but I don't want to. I love you too much, I love your heart and soul, I love your family, I love everything about you that makes you who you are. You're my soulmate, my best friend, my confidence, my lover, my crush, my team mate, my work partner, my bridge to Jesus. Jessica, you're my everything.

I know I've made a mess of everything and for that I'm sorry. I don't really know where to go from here, and to tell you the truth, I really don't care. I don't care where we live, I don't care what we do, I don't care how we get there, all I know is I want to get there with you. And for once in my life I have the faith that no matter what happens we're going to make it if we stick together. I want to share a life with you, I want to live my life for you, I want to have kids with you, I want to be holding your hand when I die beside you.

After reading the letter you gave me on my birthday, I must pick out a couple issues. Stop being so hard on yourself. You're not in the wrong, I am. The only thing that hurt me was that you compared me to all those other people. I'm my own person. I didn't choose the cards I was given in this life, yes my dad* was

---

*(Ronnie's birth father, Ron)

an addict and alcoholic, and yes that probably means genetically I probably am too. Neither of those things I can change. Yes, I was affected immensely by his death, by my parents' divorce, by past relationships that have failed me, and especially by years of drug abuse, alcohol abuse, and an overdose, all of which I did to myself. It's an understatement if I said I didn't have a little rust, but you know me, you know my heart, you know my nature, and I would hope you know I'm not just like every other person in the world who has thrown their life away. I don't want to throw my life away. I want to live my life with you, I want to have kids, I want a house in Bowness with a yard and BBQ where I can make dried out chicken for everyone after church on Sunday afternoons with the Dolphins playing on the TV. I'm not perfect, there are going to be times when you're going to want to give up on me, times where you're disappointed in me, and frustrated, but I pray that during those times there's enough hope that you continue to stick it out with me. I also know it's not always going to be a walk in the park but I'm up for the challenge. I can't wait to make you the happiest girl in the world.

I know you said in the letter that you gave to me after you moved out that next time I come back to you I better be ready to settle down and ready to give you a ring. I don't have a ring but I am offering this:

Trip for two, you and me, to New York in the fall like we've always talked about. I know you've really wanted me to go on a couple's trip with you and I think it's time. Plus, I know how bad you want to go to New York. And I promise it won't be all about sports. If you're willing to give me another chance (I know

111

I've already gotten way too many) I would love to take you to New York. I would love to come back into your life and love you like Jesus does with a love that is patient and kind, a love that is not jealous nor boastful or proud or rude. It does not demand its own way. It is not irritable and it keeps no record of being wronged. It does not rejoice about injustice but rejoices when the truth wins out. Love never gives up, never loses faith, is always hopeful and endures through every circumstance. That's the kind of love I want to show you . . .

Jessica, you finished your last letter off to me with "Willing to work at this, and I want to spend the rest of my life with you" if those words are true, then please forgive me for everything; let's start fresh and honour God for all the hard work He has done trying to keep us together and for getting us together in the first place. I love you with my whole heart and soul; you're my baby girl and always will be.

Ronnie

As the sun dropped behind the tall buildings of the Calgary skyline, we kissed on the back of that tailgate. I didn't doubt for a second that this was it. I was going to marry Hot Ronnie, and we were going to make it through—no matter what. He drove me home and asked if he could take me out for Stampede, and without hesitation, I said yes. I threw on a dress, grabbed my cowboy boots and a hat, and raced back to the truck. When we got to the grounds, we were headed to his little sister's grandstand show.

Ronnie was looking for his dad Jimmy when he spotted us. He came running down the stands and asked if we were finally back together. I smiled, and he picked me up and twirled me around. We found the rest of the family and told them the good news. Things just felt different. Over the next week of Stampede parties, Hot Ronnie proudly showed me off and never forgot to introduce me. He barely had a drink and didn't leave my side. We stayed up late and listened to country music till the wee hours of the morning. We decided our song was "Springsteen" by Eric Church; it had just been released and felt so right.

* * *

On Wednesday September 26, 2012, we flew out to NYC. I had dreamed of this moment since I was a little girl. Ronnie had taken care of all the travel arrangements, and I just had to show up. I had a hunch I might come home from this trip with something sparkly on my hand, but we would have to see about that.

The first morning in NYC I was up by 6:00 a.m. and on a subway to the Financial District to take a SoulCycle class. Poor Ronnie had no idea where I was, but I couldn't help myself. New York is not a city to relax in; it is a city to explore and see and do. When I finally got back to the hotel, we had an epic fight about the United Nations. It was silly and made me doubt that he was going to propose. Later that day, we were able to laugh it off. We also couldn't stop laughing at the horrible jeans Hot Ronnie picked up in Calgary that were four sizes too big for him and made him look like Puff Daddy from a 1990's music video. I took him shopping because I was not going to be caught dead hanging out with him in those jeans. That night, we got ready for dinner. Hot Ronnie had on his new outfit. We went for drinks on the rooftop of our hotel before we headed off to walk to the restaurant. We held hands, and he squeezed me tight.

We ate at Quality Meats, which sounds terrible but it was beyond fantastic (sorry to my vegan friends). The food was some of the best I have ever tasted. The restaurant was really crowded, and I partly hoped that the proposal wasn't going to be in front of everyone, so when the bill came and we paid and left, I knew I was in the clear. We strolled down the street to Central Park and found a horse drawn carriage. We hopped in. It was slightly starting to mist but we didn't care. The ride lasted for what felt like thirty seconds and when Ronnie got out and paid the guy, I saw Ronnie pass over $200 cash. The driver took off like a rocket, and I looked at Hot Ronnie in shock, "Did you just give that guy $200 for that short ride?" Poor guy was so nervous he totally panicked and couldn't count the bills. We still laugh about that to this day.

In Central Park, Hot Ronnie scampered up a hill and peed on a tree. I was mortified. This is Central freaking Park! Who pees on a tree? Clearly, this was no longer the night he was proposing. But seconds later, we were walking on Bow Bridge and no one was around. He dropped to one knee and started saying all these amazing things I waited my whole life to hear. I just kept interrupting him saying "Uh huh, yeah," trying to rush along the impending question. He finally just said "Screw it!" and asked "Will you marry me?"

I think I blurted "Yes," quickly followed by, "Did you get me the ring I wanted?" What a brutal response! He still bugs me about it to this day. We cried and hugged and found a random passerby to take our picture eventually. It was romantic and perfect and one of the best moments of my life. We found another rooftop bar and celebrated, then headed back to our hotel and celebrated again, falling into bed with smiles on our faces. The rest of the trip was incredible. I loved traveling with Ronnie—he made me feel loved and taken care of and completely safe.

One of my favourite memories from the next day was when he took me shoe shopping. Macy's was having some insane sale. At one point, I must have had fifteen plus shoe boxes open. We had been there for several hours, and I could tell that Hot Ronnie was starting to get hangry and he was a little over the shoes. I told him I could come back later myself, and he looked at me and said, "You like all of these?" And then looked at our sales associate and pointed out his favourite seven pairs that fit me and asked her to wrap them up. I think every girl dreams of being spoiled like this. It was my *Pretty Woman* moment.

It was the trip of a lifetime.

* * *

Ok, here's the deal: I did not decide to trust my gut and take Ronnie back because I was desperate. I made that decision to be with him from a place of strength. I took him back, but I did it when I was strong and solid, not when I was weak and scared.

When we make decisions out of fear, we can't experience the fullness of joy that life has to offer. When we live out of scarcity, we tell ourselves that we are not enough, and that there is not enough love to go around. As a result, we take the scraps we are given, but we are never filled. I was living out of fear and scarcity the first year and a half that Ronnie and I were dating. He wasn't loving me the way I craved to be loved, and he wasn't treating me the way I deserved to be treated. But I took the scraps and crumbs that he gave me because I was scared to lose him, and I tried to convince myself it was enough.

When we broke up, I started to realize that I can love myself the way I crave to be loved, and I can treat myself the way I deserve to be treated—there's no scarcity because it comes from inside me, it comes from God whose love knows no limits. During this season, my picture of love became stronger and less riddled with insecurities. I was able to wholeheartedly say yes to Ronnie when he asked me to take him back and when he asked me to marry him because I was living and making decisions out of abundance and strength. I had never been more joyful.

Making decisions out of abundance is the only way to live a full and joyful life. Living out of abundance means we know our worth isn't dependent on the decisions that we make. It means that we know we are enough and that we are aware of and thankful for the strength that we have. In order to live out of abundance, we need to make sure we aren't feeding ourselves scraps and crumbs; we need to speak love to ourselves daily and realize the plentiful gifts, talents, and blessings that we have. Stop eating scraps when there's a feast in front of you!

THE NUDGE:

Living out of abundance means making thousands of little, daily choices. It might be a nudge to be kind to yourself when you look in the mirror, or the nudge to take a minute to reflect on something you achieved that you're really proud of (even if it happened in high school; there's no time limit here). Maybe it's a nudge to take some time for yourself to give yourself the rest that you need. When those daily choices come up, start asking yourself, "How can I live in abundance?"

THE CHOICE:

When we choose to take care of ourselves, trust ourselves, and love ourselves, we will be more able to let go of anyone or anything that hinders us from fully realizing our worth. When new opportunities come up or people come back into our lives, we are then able to respond out of abundance rather than scarcity or desperation. Choose to be around people that enhance and encourage that abundance rather than people who limit it.

THE JOY:

Joy comes when you find strength on your own. You are in control of your life. Make sure that you prioritize yourself and make time to check in with yourself to see if anyone or anything is getting in the way of you loving yourself for who you are. You deserve the best; sometimes loving who you are now is all you need to bring the joy.

STUBBORN IN LOVE

the nudge to find a real problem

Wedding time! Okay, this time, I'm talking about my wedding.

Hot Ronnie and I got married on my parents' farm. It was beyond special to be able to get married on a piece of land my parents have poured so much into. My mom and friends DIYed their hearts out to make it look like it was straight out of a magazine. It was beyond better than my expectations. The décor, the BBQ food, the weather and how many of our friends traveled from afar to be there. It was a sunny day, Saturday, July 20, 2013. Our ceremony was in the middle of a wheat field, and my mom had sewn custom covers for straw bales everyone sat on so no one was uncomfortable. Literally, right before the ceremony the clouds parted. When I walked down the aisle surrounded by 285 of our closest family and friends, I knew this was it. I didn't doubt it for a second. I couldn't wait to call Hot Ronnie my husband. Our close friend Godwin married us. During our vows, I promised to cheer for the Miami Dolphins, regardless of how bad they are, and Ronnie called me his angel sent from God.

We sealed the deal with a kiss and then ran down the aisle to a Keith Urban song to kick off the party. Our guests played croquet, cornhole, bocce, and danced the night away. Ronnie and I had so much fun that we decided to cancel our honeymoon and stay back and visit with friends who travelled from around the world.

My favourite picture from the wedding is a photograph of my father-in-law, Jimmy, with his shirt off and his hands in the air, smiling as we unloaded straw bales for the reception set-up. Jimmy was always happy, always happy to help and so willing to do what it took. One of the most memorable parts of that day was the speech he gave. He didn't like crowds or to be the centre of attention, but he stood up and told the entire room he knew from the moment he met me that I was the one for Ronnie. We have those words recorded in our wedding video, and I play it often to hear his voice. Jimmy passed away six months after our wedding. He was such a strong pillar in our relationship, and I'm so grateful that I had the opportunity to know him. I love looking at that shirtless photo of him from our wedding because it brings me so much joy. It captures him perfectly: hard-working, kind, caring, and willing to do anything for anyone all while enjoying the sunshine and getting an epic tan.

The late summer days after the wedding passed by in a blur, and by September, we were all trying to get back into a normal rhythm. But in the first year of marriage, "normal rhythm" just doesn't exist. Ask anyone and they will tell you—it's a myth. If you think you achieved "normal rhythm" in your first year of marriage, congratulations, but I don't think we can be friends. If you are married, you know that marriage is hard work. I mean really hard work. You have to work at it daily. In that first year, I began learning that if you are not growing together, you are growing apart.

* * *

Almost exactly a year after our wedding, I turned thirty. And my thirtieth birthday SUCKED! I couldn't sleep that night. I tossed and turned, the bed was terrible, the pillows were like rocks, it was hot and humid, and I could not get comfortable. So finally, at about 4:30 a.m., I called my husband. Yeah, I called him. He wasn't beside me. I didn't just roll over and wake him up because I had taken off without telling him in an attempt to run away from my problems.

Before I dialed his number, I saw the text message he sent at 12:01 a.m. exactly on my birthday: "Happy Birthday. Can't believe you're not here. I really hope 30 is better for you than 29 was. Miss you and love you. Wish you were in my arms." A good sign, I guess. He said he loves me and wishes I was in his arms. It could be worse.

Year thirty on paper should be better than twenty-nine. I was married, we had started the process of making a baby, I had a new job, I owned fabulous shoes, Ronnie had just got his business underway, and the future was looking bright. Things were looking up. Or so we thought.

4:30 a.m., and I heard him pick up on the other end of the line.

"I can't sleep anymore; can you sing me a song?" Ronnie used to sing me to sleep when we were dating. I always ask him to sing for me when I can't sleep or tell me stories about history. I opted for a song this time; history would have been too heavy.

Where was I even calling him from, you might be asking. I was staying with my parents for refuge and barely speaking to Ronnie. My bank account balance was at -$356.71. Our mortgage was due tomorrow morning, and I had no idea where the money was going to come from.

How did we get here? Why wasn't I in my husband's arms on my birthday? Why was I tossing and turning on a bed with springs poking into my back? Would you believe me if I told you the answer to these questions had to do with plumbing? (If you're married, you probably believe me . . .)

A week before my infamous thirtieth birthday, we returned home after a four-week vacation with Hot Ronnie's grandparents in Europe. It was insane. We quickly unzipped our suitcases and collected our things to do laundry. Ronnie threw in the first load, which annoyed me because I had said I would do our laundry together. It was like he didn't even hear me; he just started washing his clothes without me.

Here's the deal: I like to sort my clothes: whites, lights, coloureds, darks, and even separate my Lululemon items to ensure they last longer. And he just threw everything in the wash, which peeved me to no end. The fight was on. *Fine, don't listen,* I thought to myself. Then I opened my mouth when I should have just let it be and done my laundry the next morning.

"I feel like you never listen to me," I snapped. "I just told you I would do the laundry and then you go and start yours without even asking if I have anything. What are you thinking?"

"Nothing! What is your problem? I am just getting it done."

"My problem is that you never listen to me, I can never do anything right for you. I am trying to do something sweet. I like doing laundry."

Moments later our house sitter came by and said, "I just wanted you to know that your water has backed up when you were gone. I got my friend to come by and take a look and he thinks maybe to get a plumber in. Not sure. I haven't really been using a lot of water."

"Okay, I am sure it is nothing."

After sitting for twenty minutes, I felted nudged to make sure the water situation was okay.

"Excuse me, I am just gonna double check the laundry."

Within less than twenty seconds, I was screaming up to Ronnie and the house sitter Julie to come and help with the laundry. Water was coming up everywhere in our laundry room.

It was a total nightmare. We started cleaning up water with towels and our wet vac, and I quickly got on the phone with an emergency plumber. They came and sorted things out, and when it was time to pay, none of our credit cards worked. They were maxed out from the trip, and the bill was well over $1000. Unfortunately, Hot Ronnie and I were not the saving types, and we had overspent during the last four weeks. We were totally drained. It is beyond embarrassing to even have to type this. We used our housesitter's card to pay the plumber and promised to pay her back.

The following Monday was a holiday for most, but I decided to go into the office to catch up after vacation. My work situation had changed a bit. I was no longer at Jugo Juice because I had been recruited and decided to follow my friend Carrie to a massive software company. But it was not all sunshine and rainbows at the new job. Before I left on our trip, some crap hit the fan, and my integrity was being questioned. The last thing I wanted was for this new company to question my integrity. It is one of my most valued characteristics.

So, I went in on the holiday Monday to get a head start and get prepared. I was the only idiot downtown that day. As I was going through emails and reading rude comments from the VP, I thought to myself. *Why am I here? I hate it here. Like totally hate it. I don't believe in the product—the majority of the time the software didn't even work, and the industry I am dealing with has nothing to do with what I am passionate about.* I decided to stop complaining and just press on, but the nudge on my heart to get out wouldn't go away. I was beyond miserable. I came home grumpy, tired from the jetlag and dreading work the next day. When I arrived home, Ronnie announced that the plumber was back and our bill would be about $18,000 because they had to dig up the driveway and fix the pipe. Holy hell.

"SORRY, WHAT?!"

Hot Ronnie and I were at each other. There was nothing we could do, so we went to bed frustrated and grumpy, blaming each other for this terrible situation for which neither of us were really to blame.

The next day, I rose early and was at the office just after 7:00 a.m. But by 7:30 a.m., I found myself saying that I will be damned if this is my life. I thought to myself, *I turn thirty in four days, and I hate my life. I hate going to work, the environment is toxic, I am not valued here, the work is pretty meaningless. To have my integrity questioned when it is what I pride myself on is a gut-wrenching feeling.* And so just like that, I wrote up a letter of resignation for my boss by 7:35 a.m., waited for him to arrive, and handed it to him.

"I can't do it."

He nodded and said he understood. For the record, my boss was incredible and believed in me. It was the boss above him that was making it way too uncomfortable to be there. There was no saving this—the writing was on the wall. And like that, I walked out.

Hot Ronnie and I were living paycheck to paycheck with no extra money, and as I mentioned, our trip drained our bank accounts. And now, I quit my job. I was making almost double what Ronnie made and paid the majority of our mortgage and bills.

I went home, called Ronnie, and told him I quit.

"YOU WHAT?! ARE YOU CRAZY?! That's it. I am over this. Our marriage is cursed. Nothing has gone right in this first year. It has to be a sign. Dad died, this plumbing bill, and now you quit without even consulting me or having something lined up. I am moving back to my mom's house and filing for separation. I can't do this anymore."

Those exact words were like a knife straight to my heart. They stung more than I cared to admit. Failure just about punched me in the face.

Within seconds of that phone call, I was on the phone with my parents, and an hour later I was on a flight to Winnipeg. I couldn't stand to be in Calgary at our house, seeing Ronnie's disappointment and anger with me. I feared how much worse the fight would really get. My little brother picked me up from the airport and took me for dinner, I cried the entire time and ate two orders of French fries. Talk about emotional eating. It was like I thought the greasy goodness would absorb all my fear, troubles, and sadness. (We've all been there. But if you haven't, congratulations.)

Thank God I have level headed, non-reactionary parents. Yes, they took me in amidst my distress, but the next day, it was time to work through some stuff. My parents and I got on speaker phone with Ronnie and started to talk through our situation. They calmly listened to both sides and didn't give us any answers, but merely acted as mediators. We ended the conversation on a much better note. The next day, I turned thirty—it was pretty low key and not how I dreamed up my thirtieth birthday. I spent the day taking my sweet grandma to her doctor's appointment and sulking around the farm. Not exactly how you picture celebrating a major milestone.

So that, my friends, is why I wasn't in my husband's arms on my birthday. It was all because of the dang plumbing. Well, that plus one hundred other things we wrongfully blamed each other for.

I flew back home the next day after getting a healthy dose of perspective. Ronnie and I decided a few things that day we talked over the phone with my parents. First, we would get a second opinion on the plumbing and see what was up. Second, and more importantly, Ronnie and I decided we would work on our marriage; it wasn't over. I was determined to make it work with this man. I couldn't give up on him that easily. I fought so hard to be with him, and now, I needed to use that same fight to *stay* with him. So, I arrived home and went straight to the store. I purchased all the ingredients for homemade pasta sauce and cooked one of his favourite meals. I made us re-watch our wedding video—like all four hours of it—and we made up and made a plan. It wasn't easy, but we chose to stick it out. Boy, am I'm glad we did because one week later, I peed on a stick and found out our first baby was on the way.

* * *

Looking back, I now see we encountered more in our first year of marriage than most do in five years. We went to see a marriage counsellor at the church we attended. Want to know what he told us? "Go find a real problem. This was all figure-outable."

When I look back at this period of our lives, a lot of tension came from financial strain and poor communication. Those are both big reasons why a lot of marriages fail. After one counseling session and being told to get a real problem, Ronnie and I renewed our commitment to be what we call "stubborn in love." We have been ever since that counseling session. To this day, we have not had a fight like my thirtieth birthday showdown. Now, we don't even let that mindset into our marriage. Every problem we face, we assume that we are in it together. Every tough situation or hard conversation begins from the place of: "Well, we are stuck together for another seventy years, so we better find a friggin' solution." Try it. It works.

What does it really mean to be stubborn in love? It means knowing you are on the same team. Teammates don't waste time blaming each other—they use all their effort to work toward a solution. When tough seasons come, when there are plumbing bills and dumb fights about laundry that in reality go much deeper than separating lights and darks, and your husband calls your marriage "cursed," you have a choice. You are at a crossroads. You can either throw in the towel, or you can air out your dirty laundry and decide to stick it out for seventy more years.

Getting stubborn in love takes out the possibility of giving up.

It says, "One way or another, we are getting through this together," which is terrifying yet comforting, so difficult yet abundantly joyful.

THE NUDGE:

You can make it work, but you have to put in the work. When you are fighting with your spouse, it often feels like you can never see eye to eye and that you are against each other. In reality, you are a team. When you are going through an off season, there will be nudges to show love, compassion, kindness, or vulnerability. And often—due to pride—we ignore those nudges because we are right and we need our spouse to know and admit to it. Following nudges toward humility and love is a great reminder that you are on each other's team. You are not fighting each other; you are fighting the problem—together.

THE CHOICE:

The choice you have to make is whether or not you are willing to be stubborn in love. Being stubborn in love means choosing to be allies rather than opponents, it means fighting for the other person more than fighting with them, it means having a love that is firmly rooted in character and respect and not circumstances.

THE JOY:

Life comes with its fair share of valleys and mountain tops. When you find someone who makes the lows not as low and the highs even higher, make sure you fight for them and stay on their team. There is no greater joy than having someone on your team, fighting for you and solving problems with you.

OH BABY

the nudge to recognize beauty

Monster size jars of pickles and endless amounts of grapefruit cups from Costco. Yep, those were the things I craved when I was pregnant.

After I quit my job, I was quickly able to find work and started small business consulting. I had always wanted to go out on my own but never had the courage to pursue it. I always talked myself out of really going for it because I had so many lingering fears and doubts in my mind. But now, free from the restraints of a typical nine-to-five, I was forced to make it happen. It was nothing fancy, but I picked up a few clients. One client, when they heard I was pregnant, offered to bring me on as an employee so I could qualify for maternity leave. And so, I did just that. The timing was perfect, and they let me stay until I didn't want to be on my feet anymore.

As we got closer to the birth of our firstborn, I was trying to prepare myself for birthing an *actual* human being into the world. Like first, are you serious? And second, give me all the drugs. I won't go into all the crazy details, but I will give you the short version of how this all went down. I wanted an epidural, and Ronnie didn't think it was the best idea. He told me and the nurses that *HE* would know when I'm ready. Yeah.

After our birthing class, the teacher, who was pretty hippie granola herself, told us that any drugs could really damage the baby or slow their start. Ronnie took her words to heart. On the day I went into labor, every time I asked for the epidural, he would wave off the nurse and tell them to come back in a bit.

Fair warning. Here's the part where I tell you exactly what it was like in that delivery room. When I was finally fully dilated, the nurses wanted me to hold my legs up. Well, I'm quite curvy and have some meat on me. Holding legs up after laboring for what felt like twenty-four hours was not in the cards, so I decided to take control of things. I flipped over onto my knees. I could feel that this baby was coming, and there were no delays now. I guess that is the joy of no drugs, right?

And so, on my knees, my bare ass for everyone to see, I started pushing. The doctor rushed in and looked at my husband, and said, "So, I guess we are doing it like this." The very next push was my last one and out came a beautiful baby girl. Healthy and screaming loudly, letting us know she had arrived and was earth-side.

Swayzie Grace Ronalee Olstad was born at 4:21 a.m. Funny how in the letter Ronnie wrote me during Stampede, he said the only thing anyone should be doing at 4:00 a.m. is giving birth. And here came our girl. Swayzie was seven pounds, four ounces, and beyond perfect. It was such a happy day. We called my parents first and woke them up. We had to let my mom know who our baby girl was named after. My mom Ronalee is super special to both me and Ronnie. She cares deeply for everyone, spends hours in prayer and journaling, she is patient and gracious, and always always always has room for one more at the table, no questions asked. At one point while holding our daughter, Hot Ronnie was so emotional that he almost named Swayzie just Ronalee after my mom. Swayzie was adorable, she was easy going and open to anyone holding her, loving on her, and taking care of her. This would serve us well later on.

Just like that, I was a mom. Transitioning into motherhood was pretty easy for me. I was out and about, having people over right away. Just hours after getting home, we had family arriving nonstop. Ronnie waited on me hand and foot for the first two weeks. He made fresh pressed juice for me every morning and did diaper changes and was the most amazing dad ever. He didn't waver. Times were tight, but we managed it. When you become a mother, there is no choice but to make it work. I grew a love for this sweet babe instantly and knew I would do anything to protect her, keep her safe, and give her every opportunity to be successful.

* * *

When Swayzie was about four months old, I started getting super tired again. I could barely open my eyes. Something was up. Swayzie was sleeping a full twelve hours through the night, and I was getting my rest as well. So why was I so tired? Something was just not adding up. I would fall asleep on the couch in the middle of the day with drool hanging out of my mouth because I was so tried.

I peed on a stick in October. It signaled baby number two was on the way.

Oh boy. Hot Ronnie and I were not financially or emotionally ready for another baby. And I was definitely not physically ready—it had only been four months since I pushed my first sweet, little bundle of joy out of my body. The financial strain was really stressful, and the timing was not ideal, but I knew Hot Ronnie and I would make it work—come what may. I loved being a mom and fell intro a rhythm really quickly. I got sweet Swayzie on a schedule and had a group of three other mom friends all with girls that were just six weeks apart in age. That time together was such a blessing. When you have a babe, find a tribe of women to stick it out with. Being a parent is hard work. And no matter how incredible your partner is, they just don't get it the same way a mama does. This mama group was some of the first to know that baby number two was en route, and they were nothing but the most supportive people.

On May 25, 2016, just two days before my due date, the contractions started. I forced myself to go to the gym earlier that night so I could walk this baby out. Well, you know, it was more of a waddle, and every ten minutes, I would stop to pee. It was frustrating, but I got in over an hour of walking. I was determined to have this baby early. So, at 2:00 a.m. when the contractions started, I got up and got a bowl of cereal and watched an episode of Fixer Upper that had been recorded on my DVR. I waited at home like any second-time mom would until I couldn't take the contractions anymore. I had just been at this very hospital only thirteen months earlier, so I knew all too well what to expect. No one is joking around when you hit eight centimeters dialated and the burning ring of fire is in full force. Literally Johnny Cash can take it and shove it where the sun don't shine.

When we arrived at the hospital, I was already six centimeters dilated and got escorted right into a room. When we walked in, I introduced myself to the nurse.

"Hi, I am Jess, and this is Ronnie. What is your name?"

"I'm Megan!"

"Oh okay. And how do you spell it?"

"M-E-A-G-H-A-N"

Holy Hanover, the longest way possible to spell that name. I think I gave an exasperated sigh, but I get a pass because it was just the pain from the contractions talking. I said, "You spell it however you need to. I just want to lay the ground rules so we are all on the same team here."

I let Meaghan with an extra A and H know my plan and how this would all go down. I didn't walk in with a binder of a birth plan, but I just knew it was going to be quick. I didn't want someone stroking the side of my arm telling me how awesome it was going to be. That's what the nurse did with Swayzie, and I hated it. Not her fault—poor girl was doing what she felt was best. Nothing about having that much pain felt awesome to me. Once you have your child on your chest, however, it is everything and then some. But the lead up to that moment was, uh, not awesome for me.

The game plan went like this:

"You're going to break my water with the long crochet hook and then soon after that, I will fully be dilated and the baby will be here not too long after that. I only pushed twelve times for my daughter and so I anticipate this moving at a rapid pace."

I even remember telling Meaghan, our amazing nurse, "Don't wait to page the doctor because when I say this baby is coming, I literally mean the baby is coming." She took me seriously and prepped the room for delivery. Like clockwork, after breaking my water with the long crochet hook, a fast forty-five minutes later, I was in the shower and screamed, "I have to push!"

And so, I pushed right there. I couldn't move. I was paralyzed by the urge to push. I just stood there with hot water running down my back and pushed. Let's be honest: when I pushed, I also pooped myself. See, no one ever tells you this stuff, so I feel it is my great motherly duty for those of you who have never had a baby to say that you most likely are going to shit yourself. Yes, shit in front of everyone. It's embarrassing for you in the moment, but the nurses are professionals, and you are not the first person that has shit themselves in a hospital, so get over it. I remember yelling at them, "I shit in the shower, can someone clean it up so it doesn't stink?" The team was urgently asking me to make my way to the bed, and so I did. At this point, I think I was almost buck naked. I didn't care . . . I was too hot, too sweaty, too wet from the shower to care. Just as I got back to the bed, I felt the urge to push again. And so, I did—standing up. The nurses at this point were really wanting me to get into bed and so I wobbled up there. I was kneeling at this point, my arms dangling over the top of the bed my face pushed into the pillow, butt in the air like labor number one.

"I can't do it." I yelled, even this was a little faster than I thought it was going to happen. It hurt, and I had no pain killers, no epidural. I felt like giving up. Except when you are having a baby, there is no quitting, no giving up, just more pushing.

The nurse got right in my face, just like I asked of her. There was no stroking and telling me how awesome it was. Just hardcore, sergeant-like commands. She meant business. All I can remember was her yelling in my face, saying, "Talking isn't pushing, now push!" It was exactly what I needed to hear. I pushed. And there he was.

Lewiston James Olstad in all of his glory, seven pounds, three ounces, born at 8:50 a.m., with ten fingers, ten toes, and the softest sweetest most gentle cry ever. The cry was so soft you could barely hear it. They placed him directly on my chest like I asked, and I soaked in this healthy little baby boy who was all ours. He kept crying, but I didn't mind at all, it was so sweet that I just soaked it in.

I couldn't believe we had another babe. Swayzie was only thirteen months old and had just started walking. She was not even really talking besides the occasional "puppy" and "pasta." Hot Ronnie and I soaked in those precious hours in that hospital room. We smiled at each other, not knowing how we were going to do it, but knowing we had each other and we were building a life together. Lewiston was just meant to be, even if he came way sooner than we were ready. I remember Ronnie sitting in the big chair in the corner of the room, thinking how awesome it is that we have a son and a daughter. It is truly the dream family.

We stayed in the hospital for another eight hours, and I asked to get the heck out of there. Hot Ronnie's hockey team, the San Jose Sharks, were in the Western finals, and the game was starting soon. We wanted to get back to our home, so after pushing and prodding the doctors, we got released just hours after I delivered. Lewiston was healthy, feeding well, and we really had no concerns. So off we went to go take our baby boy to meet our baby girl, whose world was about to get rocked.

There was something about Lewiston that could just draw you in. He had these big blue eyes and amazing long lashes that looked like lash extensions. I won't ever have the words to describe just how beautiful he was. He would capture your attention, and all you could see was this soul that made you want to live better, stand a bit taller, and love that much deeper. I have no idea how a baby that young could make someone feel all that, but he did.

In that moment I felted nudged to take it all in. To stop worrying and just soak up the moments because holding a new born baby doesn't last forever. All our worries about not being ready or not being in a good enough financial situation melted away. Life throws curveballs at you sometimes, and you have a choice: you can either choose to complain and focus on all the cons of the curveball, or you can choose to see the beauty in all its surprising, spontaneous glory.

THE NUDGE:

There is so much beauty in the world. It is truly all around us. It can often be hard to see the beauty when stress and busyness and unideal timing cloud your eyes. But when you get a nudge to truly look at and be in awe of the beauty in the world, follow that. Look into a beautiful baby's eyes, stop and look at the flowers on your way into work, put down your phone and savor your coffee in the morning, look at yourself in the mirror a little longer. Take in the beauty; revel in it. The beauty is there. You just need to recognize it.

THE CHOICE:

We have the choice to let the busyness and stress of everyday life sap out all the beauty, or we can let the beauty of life captivate us throughout our day-to-day lives. Yes, life is busy, stressful, and tiring. But life is also full of moments of deep connection, hope, and joy, love, and so many other beautiful feelings. We have to choose to see it though. You get to do that. You do—no one else.

THE JOY:

When we take the time to savor moments of beauty in this world, we are bringing light, hope, and peace to our hearts and also the environments we encounter. We have to adjust our eyes and our hearts to looking for beauty and moments of joy through our day rather than fixating on the hardships.

THE DIAGNOSIS

the nudge toward resiliency

You know when you're watching an Olympic track event on TV and a hurdler just wipes out?

Everything inside of you just cringes. You don't know exactly what they're going through in that moment because you, for one, haven't been training your whole life for the Olympics, but you know falling down on TV in front of the whole world must feel pretty dang brutal. You've known crumbling, you've known unmet expectations, you've known pain. Moments of crumbling are very lonely, and it makes the rest of life feel very unfocused. Like you're looking at the world through the wrong prescription and all you can see is your own brokenness. All you can see is the missed hurdle and the loss that comes with it. Moments of crumbling suck. They come out of nowhere when you least expect it. Life is just fine and dandy and then BOOM . . . Chaos. Wipeout. No possibility of a gold medal in the near future.

When Lewiston was born, I had no idea a crumbling moment was upon me. I had no idea I'd catch the hurdle on the way down and be left scraped up on the track, face down barely able to see straight, having to ask others to help me up.

We now had two babies under thirteen months. Luckily, my mom is the bomb-dot-com and stayed and helped with the crazy transition.

Hot Ronnie has always been super hands-on and he does everything: vacuums, dusts, cooks, washes the dishes, and takes care of everything in between. I wished he could stay home with me full-time, but alas, someone has to pay the bills. So, he returned to work. I just had to make it through a few weeks of being at home by myself during the day before we would take off to Winnipeg for a family vacation, where there would be lots of helping hands.

During these exhausting and overwhelming days, Lewiston began to get what I thought was extremely colicky. I held him a lot and would bounce and rock him until I couldn't stand straight anymore, and then would fall asleep with him tucked onto my chest on the couch in the living room. It was crazy.

We made it to my parents' house and enjoyed our time in Winnipeg. I planned to stay for another week or so with my parents while Ronnie left to go back to work. Lewiston was still crying lots, and I was desperate to try anything to fix his little tummy. I took him to go see a chiropractor upon a few friends' recommendations for his colic. I figured it couldn't hurt, and I was really starting to lack in the sleep department. I was staying up bouncing until eventually we passed out. I drove to the chiropractor that next morning after Hot Ronnie left. Once I got in and was brought back to the room, I took Lewiston out of the car seat, laid him on the bed, and waited patiently. Once the chiropractor came, she took one look and immediately didn't like what she saw. She said his breathing was really laboured and his skin was all mottled. I had no idea what that meant. I had not noticed his breathing at all. She suggested that I take him to Children's Emergency. She told me not to panic, but that I should really have him looked at by a doctor. I thanked her, I left her office, and I immediately called my mom. My friend Betty dropped everything she was doing to go watch Swayzie, and my mom planned to meet me at the hospital.

I had no idea how long it would take. I figured it would be a full-day affair before I got in to see a doctor. Before going to the hospital, I stopped for a coffee and gluten-free sandwich at my favourite gluten-free bakery in Winnipeg. This was just going to be a routine check, and I would rather be safe than sorry and have good healthy food to snack on, rather than raiding a hospital vending machine. I was convinced that this was all a simple misunderstanding; Lewiston was healthy, born healthy, he didn't look sick, and I didn't really think he was limp.

Upon our arrival at the hospital, the first nurse looked at me like I was crazy, as though I was a first-time mom that was super uptight—the kind of mom that freaked out if her kid even sneezed. But after taking his sleeper off and seeing his laboured breathing, we were immediately taken back to a room.

After getting ushered back to a bigger room, the next nurse came and took a look at us. The next thing I knew she was asking me to wheel Lewiston off to yet another room. As I walked with the stroller, I looked up to see a sign that read RESUSCITATION ROOM. I went from a little curtained off area to a room with twelve doctors and nurses. They were calling for more specialists and asking if I was okay, or need a chair to sit, did I have a support system. They were poking Lewiston, and yelling out his vital statistics. It was like a scene out of *Grey's Anatomy*.

I remember finally looking around and thinking, *What the F SHARP is happening here? My son is fine. Why do we need cardiology and neurology? And why is the nurse being so damn nice to me? Why are they asking me if I am okay or if I need to sit and where my husband is, and how fast he could get here?* Hot Ronnie was back in Calgary. He had left Winnipeg the day before this occurred. He was set to open a new store the next day.

So, there I was, alone, no Hot Ronnie to comfort me, my mom still en route; I was totally puzzled and in total shock at what was happening. The doctors were still acting quickly: MRIs, CT scans, EGGs, ECGs, and ABCs (okay, this last one is not a medical term, but Lord help me—so many acronyms were being ordered, I couldn't keep it straight). You know when doctors act fast, something is seriously wrong, because in Canada, if things are not that bad, it takes a long time to get anything done medically.

They started asking questions, and I confessed that I had a couple glasses of wine almost every night at the lake while breastfeeding. And that there was this one time when his head snapped back really fast while in the carrier as it had gotten loose and was not tied up properly, and maybe that was it! Maybe I'd paralyzed him. The team assured me this was not the case. The nurse even joked with me saying having two kids under fifteen months deserved a glass of wine or two.

They continued to do tests. Finally, a nurse came out and told me to call my husband and tell him to get here as quickly as possible. I was still extremely confused. She told me Lewiston's state was not normal and that we could be in the hospital for a while figuring out what his condition was. I called Hot Ronnie. He still recalls the phone call like it was yesterday. He was at Safeway grabbing groceries in between inspections at the store so he would have some food in the fridge at home. I told him not to panic, but that the doctors and nurses said he should fly out as soon as possible. I was calm and collected. I remember this weird peace inside of me that said everything was going to be alright. Ronnie remembers having the worst feeling in the pit of his stomach. He dropped his grocery basket on the floor still filled with food, the veggies flew out all over the floor. He called his brother Tanner to come over to help him stay focused and book flights. Ronnie was at the airport within one hour and on his way back to Winnipeg.

The doctors ran every test you can think of and then some. We met with geneticists and the head of pediatrics and asked a million questions. Lewiston looked pretty good and didn't require oxygen but was still extremely limp. I wanted out of there. The one test that I had ordered was for Spinal Muscular Atrophy or SMA. Remember those two awesome kids Ishan and Shanaya? I remembered their condition and thought I should ask for our own son to be tested for it. The geneticist had said there was a small possibility that's what it could be, so I made note of that little nudge.

The neurologist had even mentioned SMA on one of the first days but then told us, and I quote, "I am 99 percent sure that it isn't SMA." Hot Ronnie and I remember high fiving when he told us that. We thought we had dodged a bullet because we knew how serious the disease was. Still, we had no answers. We were told it could be a vitamin deficiency, Lyme disease, muscular dystrophy, meningitis, or a bacterial infection. They really had not narrowed it down much.

But to be safe, I wanted to be 100 percent sure it wasn't SMA. I was all too familiar with the disease. And I wanted it completely ruled out.

You want to know the craziest part of our story? Three weeks before our "holiday" to Winnipeg, I went to the bank to get a check for $44,983.00, which I had helped raise for Ishan and Shanaya's new wheelchair-accessible van. My goal was to complete this fundraiser before Lewiston was born, but we didn't quite make our deadline. We did endless fundraisers and tried whatever we could to get people to donate to the GoFundMe. It was a grind, but we got them the money they needed. The first fundraiser I did for them, thirteen people showed up and we raised $640. Anyway, back to this SMA testing. I demanded it be done, and so they ran the test. Or so we thought.

I was in the room in Winnipeg when they drew the blood. I remember waiting twenty-four hours before we drew the blood because we had already hit the limit for blood withdrawals on a new baby. I watched them label the vial, and I remember asking them to put a rush on the test. Lewiston was only two months old at this point. I remember this all so clearly. They explained that Winnipeg didn't have a lab for this test, but I said test anyway. I even offered to pay for the test. I just wanted to be sure this was not our story. I wanted physical proof we could rule this out.

But deep in my belly I knew. I knew Lewiston didn't have a virus, or an infection, or lyme disease, but SMA. It just takes that one blood test to confirm it. They sent off the blood work and told us we would get the results back in Calgary. After six exhausting days in the hospital in Winnipeg, sleeping on a chair with Hot Ronnie at my feet and Lewiston in my arms, we still had no answers, and they discharged us.

We got back to my parents' farm, took a day to collect ourselves, and then received approval to fly home. The hospital in Winnipeg sucked the life out of me, and I wanted to get my bearings. I needed fresh air after almost a week under the bright, fluorescent lights.

Summers in Winnipeg are beautiful, and the sunsets are better than anywhere. There's nothing quite like a prairie sunset. The sun drops behind the flat fields that my parents have poured their blood, sweat, and tears into for over forty years. So that night before heading home, my mom and I went out for a walk to watch the sun fall behind their beautiful crop.

"It's SMA," I whispered. Tears slowly fell down my face, my bottom lip quivered, and in that moment, I was scared.

"How do you know? Why are you so certain?" my mom asked.

"It's his thumb." I replied.

"His thumb?"

"Yes, his thumb. It does the same thing Ishan and Shanaya's thumbs do. I just know it."

And with that little nudge, one that I would have much rather lived without, we made our way home, anxious for whatever news we would find out about Lewiston. Upon landing, we got a call from the Alberta Children's Hospital saying they wanted to see us immediately. They had gotten a few pieces of our file and some things concerned them, but they encouraged us to go to our doctor first. We went to our family doctor, and she said that this was not the same baby she saw at one month old. She sent us straight to Alberta Children's Hospital.

The Winnipeg hospital caught up the team in Alberta with all that had gone on and sent our records to give them a heads up about what we were dealing with. We were admitted right away, and more testing began. Our medical records were transferred, and we found out that the hospital staff in Winnipeg never sent off the blood work for SMA testing. They claimed they didn't draw the blood, and as a result, we would have to do several of these painful tests over again.

In the midst of all this, I made our journey public on my Instagram account. I wasn't concerned with who or how many people were following along, but I needed a space to share the thoughts swimming through my brain. It was then that people started following and listening, and I just shared in a real and raw way. Even to this day, those posts are still messy, and raw, and filled with spelling errors and missing words. The only reason this book doesn't have typos like that is is because I paid a lot of people to make sure it didn't. And let's be honest, I am sure there are one or two mistakes, and I am okay with that because, like me, it doesn't have to perfect. People knew my heart then and know it now.

And that's when the well wishes started pouring in. People said stuff like, "We are praying for you," or "Don't worry, my daughter had the same thing, and she is fine now," or my favourite one is, "Maybe it is just gas." We prayed for Lewiston's symptoms to be the result of a vitamin deficiency, or some bacterial infection that could be treated with antibiotics. We got well wishes from around the world. Mine and

Ronnie's favourite we receieved was "We are sending love." Ronnie, to this day, asks how people send love when they don't actually physically send you anything. Like do they bottle it up and put it into a jar or envelope?

On August 5, 2016, two days before my thirty-second birthday, we were waiting in our room in Alberta Children's Hospital. The blinds were drawn, the room felt dull, it was clean and everything was in its place. We were trying to let Lewiston rest, as I was praying rest would cure him. Dr. Jean Mah, the pediatric specialist at Alberta Children's Hospital, walked into the room and dropped the bomb that she was certain our son Lewiston had SMA Type 1 and likely wouldn't make it to his first birthday.

"Sorry what?! SMA—I know it, I look after kids with SMA. They are alive, they are teenagers, they just need wheelchairs, they can't walk, but they made *their* first birthdays and then some." Little did I know that SMA Type 2 is a totally different ball game than Type 1. Type 1 is the most severe form of SMA, and given how early Lewiston was showing signs, there wasn't much hope. There was no treatment at the time and no cure.

I crumbled, there in that dark room, the blinds shut, the machines still beeping and buzzing, that depressing moment—I F'ing crumbled. I could barely breathe. Every ounce of hope we had, every belief that we were going to be okay was just robbed from us. I lay on the floor and sobbed.

Our son was dying and wouldn't make it to his first birthday.

We were just waiting on a blood test to have it confirmed and printed on a piece of paper to make it official. There was no cure, no treatment. It was just a waiting game for death. In that moment, there was darkness. No light, just utter cold and lonely darkness. *God, where are you? How could you do this? How could you let this happen? How is there even a God?*

Once the shock and news settled, Hot Ronnie and I looked at each other and made a pact right then and there that we would not let this destroy us and that we would bring joy regardless of how dark it was. We would use Lewiston's life to glorify God. Even though I wanted to punch God directly in the face.

* * *

On August 11, we went back to the hospital. I knew that there was no miracle surprise or "Whoops, sorry we got it wrong." It was just a matter of time before the SMA diagnosis was official. We walked down the hall and sat in the room waiting for the doctor to deliver the horrible news. We got the stupid piece of paper to confirm our fears. I still have it buried in Lewiston's collection of things. A bunch of medical jargon I can't understand, but basically a death sentence printed on an 8½" x 11" piece of white paper with an official lab logo. That day sucked. I shared this on my Instagram page that day.

On August 11, 2016 I wrote this:

UPDATE ON LEWISTON // Grab a box of tissue this one ain't easy. Our fears were confirmed today during our meeting with the Pediatric Neurologist at AB Children's Hospital. In Winnipeg we feared this diagnosis but were led to believe it wasn't even a possibility. Today the scary diagnosis of SMA— Spinal Muscular Atrophy Type 1 was confirmed. So, here is the crazy thing to this all. Most of you who read this will have no clue what SMA is {I put a link in my bio to read more on it} And those that have heard of it may be because you know of Ishan and Shanaya—you have donated money to help them buy a wheelchair-accessible van, been to my spin fundraisers, donated cash to our baby pool and just gave because you knew the cause was near and dear to my heart. We felt led to journey alongside a family who needed some extra care. It is so crazy for us to know so intimately how horrible and challenging this diagnosis can be. What we could have never even fathomed possible for our family is now our reality. Lewiston has been diagnosed with SMA Type 1. His life expectancy is less than two years and because he has displayed signs so early on, they are preparing us for less than a year. Stop and breathe here . . . So for now he is stable and we hope for few good months ahead before breathing and eating become our biggest challenges. We are gonna make these months count. And we will not lose all joy because of the cards our family has been dealt. There currently is no cure for SMA. Ronnie and I are still in shock, and today I am surprisingly okay and holding it together. We have had an overwhelming response of friends and family asking how they can help. I don't want to ask for help but knowing the road ahead we will need it. So, we will graciously accept it . . . In a couple of days something will be shared with more details on how. For now, we are just trying to get our feet underneath us. Praying for a miracle for Lewiston. We will be trusting steadily in God for peace, strength, and purpose. Just because we didn't get the answer we wanted from all your prayers doesn't mean good can't come from this. Continue to lift us up. We will need you in days ahead.

What major foreshadowing in my life. I had to remind myself in that moment: just because we didn't get what we wanted doesn't mean that good can't come from this. Lord, have mercy.

After getting discharged from that hospital visit, we were able to be at home. One day, several weeks after we left the hospital, I took Swayzie and Lewiston to a park. Totally manageable right? It was mid-September. A cool day, we had layers on and had just finished exploring. As we were returning to the car, Lewiston turned completely blue in his car seat right after his NG tube feed. I started screaming for someone to call 911. We were in the parking lot of the Westin Hotel in downtown Calgary—thankfully the fire department and ambulance were only two blocks away. It was that day that Lewiston got readmitted to the hospital via ambulance with a fire truck in tow, and we never left the hospital with him again.

We would never take Lewiston back home again. Never another memory made with our family of four in our little house. No more road trips or hikes to the mountains or trips to my parent's farm. We would live in that hospital and then hospice until his last breath. I had no idea that the last outing to the park would be our last full day of freedom with our son. It would be the last day that just going to the park was an effortless, carefree activity.

During moments of life-altering hurdles—when life hits you like a freight train—it feels like you'll never be able to get up again. Life feels heavier and darker and it feels like it would just be easier to stay down. But I'm here to remind you that in brokenness, there is always healing. Fractures are an opportunity for more light to come in. Feel your pain fully—don't try to mask it. Crumble. Cry. Scream if you have to. But then, get up. You have the strength to, you know you do. You've missed hurdles before; life has tripped you up before. And you got up. Look for that something nudging you to get up and dust yourself off. The nudge is stronger than defeat. You are resilient. Sometimes, bringing the joy in the midst of your darkest days is just simply the act of getting back up. That simple move from the fetal position to your knees, your knees to your feet. Stand up. Rise up, sister. Rise on up.

THE NUDGE:

When life knocks you over, you might feel the overwhelming desire to just stay down. But amidst that feeling, you will also feel the nudge to get back up and dust yourself off. You were not just dealt a crappy hand. Those cards in your hand are not the last word on your life. The fact that you are alive today and reading this book proves your resiliency.

THE CHOICE:

Resiliency isn't like having green eyes. It isn't something that some people just inherently have and others don't. Resiliency is a choice. It's a myriad of choices made through the course of our days. Choosing to be resilient during life's small setbacks (missing the bus, losing at a board game, burning the chicken) will help give you a mindset and disposition for resiliency that will help carry you through moments of crumbling.

THE JOY:

With resiliency comes joy—the steadfast, unmoving kind. Choosing resiliency doesn't mean you have to stop grieving or that all the sudden you're ready to roll again just like the old days. You can be resilient and still have the desire to just lie down for about a month. Resiliency means that you're honest with yourself about all your feelings, that you're also ferociously seeking moments of joy and beauty amidst darkness and crumbling. Beauty and pain can coexist; grieving and joy can coexist. Trust me, it is possible.

THE PACT

the nudge to know your vision

I remember in the eighth grade when I got glasses for the first time. I hadn't realized how bad my vision was until I walked outside with my new specs. I remember thinking, "Wow, bushes are made out of a bunch of individual leaves. They aren't just a green blur." Okay, maybe it was not quite that bad, but you get the idea. Before I had glasses, it was as if God had just used the 1985 Microsoft Paint app and sloppily colored some trees really quick. After that visit to the eye doctor, my world instantly became crisp, detailed, and so much more beautiful.

It's amazing what good vision can do. When life feels blurry, messy, and unfocused, it is important to pause for a minute, regroup, and figure out what your vision for this season is. Get clear.

The same day we received the horrible diagnosis that Lewiston indeed had SMA Type 1, and that his life expectancy was less than a year, I pulled myself off that hospital room floor. I looked at Ronnie while holding Lewiston in my arms, and I said:

"Even though Lewiston's life could be short, we will make it full. He will be comfortable, he will know joy, he will know love, he will feel safe, and he won't ever be alone. I'm making the decision right now. We are going to share Lewiston's story, not only to build awareness for SMA, but to also glorify God, and to show people that they don't have to suffer in silence. I know this road is scary, but we won't do it alone. We will find community. We are going to share love and grace with all the medical staff and all the people who are intertwined in Lewiston's care, and we are going to make lasting memories. Through this journey, you and I will grow together. We will not get ripped apart. We will not let this drive a wedge between us and divide us. We are going to lean on God, we are going to pray for that healing miracle every morning and every night, but above all else, we will pray that God's will be done, and that He gets the ultimate glory."

This was our pact, our motto, our battle cry. We could have chosen to run, to hide, to shut down the world, to lock ourselves in a dark room until it was over. We could have reached for alcohol, drugs, or pills. We could have chosen to numb and dull the sharp, harsh pain and reality we were suddenly facing. We could have chosen to be angry. We could have turned away from God, and let this diagnosis really affect our relationship with Him. But we didn't. We did not let the pain win. We chose to respond in the best way that correlated with the outcome we desired. We chose to care for Lewiston like no other; to have countless dance parties; to ensure he felt safe, loved, and adored.

I am not going to sugarcoat it. Lewiston's diagnosis was a bomb that would rip most couples apart. Remember when I had to fight for Ronnie and I to stay together just as hard as I fought for him to like me? That was the same fight we needed now. We asked a friend to come and sit with Lewiston so we could go outside and get some fresh air. He was hooked up to so many things that it was easier to leave him in the room, and I needed a moment to gather myself. We went to the back of the hospital and walked the track by the playground. It looks west towards the mountains. After breathing in some fresh air and having sunshine hit our faces, we reminded each other that no matter what, we are a team. And a damn good one at that. We were going to stick together, have each other's back, and make sure that Lewiston's life would be lived joyfully. We knew that together, we could bring the joy to this painful circumstance. At the time, we had no idea how, but we were determined to figure out a way.

One day, a close friend of mine came to the hospital after Hot Ronnie and I had experienced quite a day. This day had been challenging and scary; I was drained and I just needed to smile again. And so, my friend asked her eighteen-month-old daughter Allie to show me her dance moves. She played Justin Timberlake's "Can't Stop the Feeling!" on repeat, and she just went for it. I started dancing with her and started moving Lewiston's body for him so he too could enjoy the beats. If you have ever danced and not cared for a second what anyone thought, you know it is truly the best feeling. This little dance party made me feel so good that we decided to do it every day. Every day, we would bathe our son, snuggle him tight, and once he was all dried off, we would begin our daily dance party. Every day during rounds, before rounds, after rounds, we danced. I invited everyone in who wanted to join: nurses, doctors, patients, family, friends. I'm pretty sure that we alone were responsible for making JT's release a number one single. You're welcome, JT.

Still, the days were long. I would get up between 6:00 and 7:00 a.m. I slept in the room with Lewiston (thank God for Alberta Children's Hospital and rooms with parent beds). I would wear these disgusting grey sweats that were from high school, about seven sizes too big, and a hoodie to bed. Each morning, I would roll out of bed looking like a hot mess. I was pretty spoiled because I knew someone in the hospital would usually show up with a hot Starbucks for me. I would take a few sips, check on Lewiston, and then once I knew he was good, I would hop in the shower and then put on fresh clothes and some makeup.

This simple routine made me feel ready for the day. Less lazy, less gross, less out of sorts. And more ready to tackle whatever we would face that day. That small habit of showering and making my bed daily changed my life. It seems so trivial, but it became such an important part of my day.

Then at some point between 8:00 a.m. and noon, the team would make the rounds. We had the green team. And I remember how confusing it all was. The team would present on Lewiston and provide an update on his care, next steps, current medications, and changes. A typical round would start off like this: "This is Lewiston Olstad, a male, four months of age. He is in with a rare genetic disorder: Spinal Muscular Atrophy." And then, they would say a million other massive medical terms that I could not decipher one bit. The somber mood, the terms I couldn't make sense of—this is was not what I called joyful.

One day, I had had enough. Everyone stood there with their clipboards, jotting notes and looking crazy intelligent. It was so serious and somber. Call it burn out, call it frustration, call it a divine nudge to silence all the medical jargon, but this needed to end. All I could picture was Robin Williams in *Patch Adams* making his patients laugh and enjoy life. That sweet grandma that swims in the noodles. I wanted that for my son. I wanted joy and memories in this hospital room that didn't involve clipboards. And so, I stood up to this team of medical experts and said, "My son is dying, or at least that is what is written in the charts you hold. There is not a medication, no treatment, no cure. So, if this is the case, and you are all right, can we at least make this fun? This is depressing enough. This is hard enough. I am going to read you a page from my favourite kids' book, and then you are going to speak in a language I can understand, and have a dance party."

And so it began. I read from one of my favourite children's books, *The Day the Crayons Quit*. I read them the part where the orange and yellow crayons were fighting. We laughed, and we laughed some more. And after that day, rounds changed. Each morning, I would make the medical team say what they were grateful for, or I would bring in those funny glasses with the nose and moustache and make the team do the full round looking hilarious. The mood lifted; things shifted. Why? Because we chose to bring the joy. Because even facing death, I knew it could be joyful. It didn't have to be all-consuming and depressing.

The afternoon would come and visitors would trickle in, bringing food, coffee, stuffed animals, balloons, lotions, green juices, all of it. And then we would eat dinner, and I would change back into my gross, baggy, seven-sizes-too-big sweatpants and cry myself to sleep. Some days, I would take my iPhone and listen to Lauren Daigle on repeat and just let the tears stream down. Even in the midst of bringing joy to our circumstances, it felt impossibly heavy, and I often felt like no one could understand the weight of this burden I carried. I was strong, I was positive and upbeat, but when the lights on the unit dimmed and no one was around, I would cry and cry and cry and beg God to save Lewiston. Beg Him for a miracle, for a little league game, for a solution, for more than 365 days, for something to change.

Lewiston was stable, but there was nothing more that Unit 3 and the green team could do. So, they moved us to palliative care. We thought we might be able to go home because some days, he looked so strong, but that was never the case. Above all else, we wanted joy for Lewiston. He brought us so much joy and we wanted to celebrate with him while he was alive. It didn't matter where we were. We were determined to make it great. Ronnie and I made that decision to bring joy the day the doctors delivered the news that Lewiston wouldn't make it to his first birthday, and we kept our promise.

When Ronnie and I chose the vision of joy for Lewiston's life and journey, it changed everything. Yes, we still cried. Yes, we were begging for a miracle. Yes, we were in unimaginable pain, but that wasn't the only things we focused on. It was like we went to the eye doctor for the first time and were told our vision could be better and less blurry. Joy was the lens we were choosing to look through. And when we made that choice, we saw things more clearly. We saw dance parties in the hospital room and goofy glasses on doctors. Our vision brought clarity, hope, and purpose amidst the chaos. That's what vision does. It makes what's in front of you crystal clear so you can move forward in confidence, even if the ground you walk on feels shaky.

The Bible says, "Where there is no vision, the people perish" (Proverbs 29:18, KJV). I believe this is 100 percent true. If we don't have vision during trying seasons, we wither: physically, emotionally, spiritually. Having vision is life-giving and vital in order to experience a life of unmitigated joy. Find your vision. Write it down. Memorize it. And then the most important part: live it out every damn day.

THE NUDGE:

Having vision is vital to handling life's lows. What is your vision for your life? What do you want your legacy to be? Your character and legacy aren't built in times of plenty; your character is built in trying times, seasons of walking through fire. When difficult seasons arise, what is the nudge of your heart? That nudge is a good indication of what your vision should be.

THE CHOICE:

The choice for us was either to let grief overwhelm us and be the marker of our son's life, or to choose to be joyful and celebrate the days that we got with him. Yes, we still grieved and it was painful, but in both small ways and big, we chose to let joy be the legacy of his time on earth. You have the choice during trials to have hope or not. Even the tiniest glimmer of hope can turn a bleak circumstance into an opportunity to dance and rejoice.

THE JOY:

When you have the mindset and resolve to be joyful—when joy is your default—it changes everything. It turns a cold hospital into a warm room, it turns a grim diagnosis into an opportunity for a miracle, it turns mourning into dancing. Joy is not a feeling, it's a mindset—it takes stubbornness to live out. It isn't dependent on circumstances; it's dependent on your resolve.

A USED BABY BOOK

the nudge to let people in

I am an extrovert. Shocker, I know.

I am the definition of a people person. I love to make sure everyone feels seen, everyone has fun, and everyone is fed. I love to be there for people in big ways and small. Need a ride to the airport? On it. You just had surgery and need a meal for your family? Here's a homemade dinner (like, a good one). Just got broken up with and need a shoulder to cry on? I have two. It's your birthday and you want a "surprise" birthday party? The invitations have already been sent out and the cake is ordered 'cause Lord knows I ain't gonna bake it. Anyway, you get the idea.

With this desire to help others being my default, it felt awkward to let people in, to let people help me for a change. It is so much easier to give than to receive. And as we moved into palliative care, I really had to humble myself to accept all the help people were extending to us. I know I am not the only medical mom that has felt this way. Well, accepting help was hard at first because I wanted to be strong and self-sufficient, God nudged me and said, "You, Jessica, are not a burden. Just as you love taking care of people and showing them kindness and love, so others love to do that for you. Rest in my provision." And that really changed my outlook.

Hot Ronnie and I kept our pact to bring the joy and to fight for our family, and we made every moment count. Our community came alongside us in a big way. I even had a group called the "Love for Lewiston Crew" who organized meals, house cleaning, yard work, fundraisers, massages, and workouts in hospice. They kept us going. I can't even count how many friends and family members would drop off hot Starbucks. Sometimes over four beverages in a day would show up. I literally could have had an IV line with Starbucks. These cups of coffee were my love language and were the best way for people to show up and let us know they cared. A simple four-dollar upside down Americano with cream and cinnamon dolce sprinkles on top made all the difference. Hot coffee is a simple yet effective way to say you love someone (that is, if they like coffee).

So, fueled by caffeine and community, we faced the long road ahead of us. It was exhausting (hence all the coffee), but we made Lewiston's life matter. We documented all of the moments, and our photographer who did his newborn photos (Liz of Spruce and Sparrow) ended up visiting us frequently to capture his life—our life—regardless of how messy and un-picture perfect it felt. She captured it perfectly. And she never asked for anything in return. She just showed up ready to serve. I love looking back at the videos and pictures, and I always smile seeing my son's sweet face. As I relive the moments, my longing for him deepens, but those pictures and videos also bring memories back of the joy and the time we did have together. They always remind me that Lewiston lived big.

We dreamed him up a bucket list and made sure he lived it out. He went on a pseudo trip to Vegas with the nurses; he had snowball fights, and felt the first snowflakes of winter; we dressed him up as Scuba Steve, a fighter pilot, and superman for Halloween—all in the same day. He even proposed to his favourite nurse and "got married."

He gave her a ring pop ring to make it official, and the nursing staff made a marriage certificate. When we committed to bringing the joy, we were not kidding around.

When I made our journey public on Instagram, so many people reached out to me, even people I didn't know that well. For instance, I knew this girl who attended my spin class, and in no way would I have said she was a good friend of mine. We had grabbed a coffee once after class, but that was it. I don't know what about our story exactly hit her so hard, but she showed up in a big way for my family, and to this day we have remained the closest of friends. You see, she saw something in how we were choosing to walk through this experience, and she decided to show up and help. On one of our darker days in the ICU, she surprised us with Dean Brody, the country singer, and he performed a private concert for us right in Lewiston's room.

On that day, I was trying to send my mom to go and get food. I only ate at the hospital cafeteria a handful of times. Having normal food was what kept me sane. The food is not the hospital's strong suit. Yes, hospitals do a lot of good, but food ain't one of them. I was hungry and wanting take-out from one of my favourite restaurants. I couldn't leave, as Lewiston wasn't doing the greatest. My mom wasn't leaving, and it was really pissing me off. She finally left to pick up my food, but then I caught her in the hallway chatting with a nurse. Little did I know that moments later, the most handsome cowboy with his hat, boots, jeans (obviously), and guitar walked into the room. My mom knew about this surprise, which is why she wasn't leaving. Dean Brody snagged a stool and began playing songs off his new album and, of course, a few of his old hits. We took pictures and got to escape the darkness for a bit. Lewiston got front row seats to an amazing country concert that night. I'm pretty sure that was on all of our bucket lists: attend a concert and sit front row. I can't thank my friend Jodie enough for making that evening possible. It was the fuel we needed. She constantly brought awesome home cooked meals and fresh baked gluten free muffins to keep me going.

We continued to implement those daily dance parties to Justin Timberlake's "Can't Stop the Feeling!" and would have nurses, staff, doctors, and even the head of maintenance join us. It was the best part of each day. It brought smiles to everyone, and was a daily ritual that we all looked forward to. Joy was hard to find some days, so we took it upon ourselves to create it. It was a choice, and that is what I believe kept us upright on the journey. Choosing to bring joy every damn day, no matter how dark the days felt.

Those four months in the hospital and hospice changed me. Because on August 5, 2016, the day Lewiston was diagnosed, after my pity party, I was so damn determined to find the light that we didn't have that day. If this had been my diagnosis, I would want to live, and live the hell out of life. We fought hard for our son. But we always said, "We fight if he has fight, but if he doesn't have fight left, we will let go and let him go."

Our fight was big, we rallied the troops. We were hoping for a miracle and researching trial treatments for SMA Type 1. We applied for every trial possible; we called drug companies endlessly and sent hundreds of emails with no replies. I called and connected with SMA parents from around the world.

The outpouring of love for our family was off the hook. People who have never even met us have blessed us. It was crazy. We were given money, clothes, free yoga, the private country concert, stuffed animals, sleepers, cool shirts, a tipi, salads, fresh cut veggies, gluten-free baked goods, personal notes, and enough Starbucks gift cards to keep me caffeinated and make me platinum elite, or something like that. It literally felt like Christmas morning opening up all the packages.

One of my favourite gifts we received was a very worn book. I know, doesn't sound too exciting. Contrary to my initial thoughts, the gift was beyond thoughtful. It was a book that these almost strangers had given their baby, Walker, at birth and inside was the message that Walker's parents had so thoughtfully written their precious son. Beside their note to Walker in November 2014 was a new inscription from Walker to Lewiston in November 2016. They probably envisioned this book in Walker's baby box of memories to be passed down to his own child someday, and instead they sent it to us. I can't describe how much this meant to me.

People who I didn't know or only knew from a distance followed our journey on Instagram. People like Joanna Gaines, who at one point commented that she was praying for us. Love came from all over the world. Sharing Lewiston's journey so publicly came naturally for me. Sharing Lewiston with the world just felt right. We had nothing to hide, nothing to be ashamed of. I wanted to let others know that death can be embraced. That joy was possible even with death knocking at our door.

I wish Lewiston could have talked; I wish I could have heard his voice. I wish I could tell him all of the things I dreamed of for his life. I wish so many things. I wanted other parents to know that as hard as parenting is, their screaming kids were actually a blessing. That wrestling to have to change a diaper or that kid walking out of his bedroom for the ninth time at bedtime, as annoying as it is, is a blessing; that it is beautiful that they can walk and talk, even if it is them talking back to you. I often find myself wanting to rip out my hair from my own precious babes driving me nutty. But I wanted parents to know that I know too many parents right now that would give anything for their child to scream at them, to smudge the mirror with the greasy, messy little hands, to color all over the table, counter, or couch. To slam the door or not flush the toilet for the millionth time. Because you know what? All these things that drive us crazy are the blessings that many other parents pray and beg for. All the crazy means we have healthy, happy children. WHAT A FREAKING BLESSING!

Becoming a medical parent gives you perspective you shouldn't have to have. And I wanted to share that. I wanted people to find joy and gratitude if their story looked like mine or if it couldn't be further from mine. Through social media, I felt like I was able to be there for others a little bit. I could share Lewiston with people, and I know I'm a little biased, but he is one of the greatest gifts of all. And by letting people in, I allowed them to be there for me in big and small ways.

Through this, I learned that community isn't only a concept or word that gets thrown around in church a lot and said so many times it starts to lose meaning. Community is a support system that can be there for you, rain or shine. True community can mean people praying with you, but it also means people bringing you ice cream if you had a hard day (or wine if you had a *really* hard day). These are people who will speak truth to you, get mad with you, make you laugh your ass off on days where you haven't even cracked a smile. Letting people into your life in all its beautiful mess is one of the most joy-producing things you can do—it creates a depth that you can't manufacture.

THE NUDGE:

A support system of people who love and care about you is like a lighthouse in a horrifying storm. They guide you toward hope. They help you see the light, stay grounded, and chart your course when the darkness is overwhelming. When storms come, it is easy to hide and try to solve problems and figure things out on your own. It seems as if it will be less painful, in a way. Let me tell you that it is not. Having people around you to hold you up when life keeps knocking you down is a game changer. When storms come—in whatever shape, form, or severity—answer the nudge to reach out and ask for help.

THE CHOICE:

You can choose to be prideful and take care of everything on your own when crap hits the fan, or you can let people into the mess, the grief, the hardship and let them help you. Accepting gifts, love, and support from people is really hard for me, but when I realized that there was absolutely no way that Ronnie and I could do this only with our own strength and with our own resources, I chose to open my hands and open my heart.

THE JOY:

There is so much joy and hope to be received when accepting support from people. And when it is your turn to be the lighthouse in someone else's storm, there will be joy in that as well.

FIGHT FOR LEWISTON'S LIFE

the nudge to choose movement

During our stay at the hospice center Lewiston was in, we had to make some pretty brutal decisions. This medical treatment or that medical treatment. This medicine or that. Mind you, I never went to medical school, nor had I learned to speak medical jargon ever before in my life. I had doctors literally laugh in my face when I told them I was holding out hope for Lewiston to make a full recovery. We were struggling with what to do and what was next.

Thankfully we were able to lean on our friend Shailynn. When we were still on Unit 3, this beautiful blonde-haired girl rolled into our room. I had never met her before, but she had heard of our story through Facebook, Instagram, and the news. Shailynn was nineteen at the time and had SMA Type 2. It was crazy the connection she had with Lewiston. We instantly hit it off, and if I had a question, concern or didn't understand all the medical crap, she was one of my first calls. We have since developed a beautiful relationship—she is like a sister to me, and I totally treat her like one too. I am hard on her and love her deeply with a fierce passion to see her grow into who she dreams of being. Shai has become a staple in our lives, and we made sure our home is wheelchair friendly as she visits often. She has been a great source of knowledge and wisdom for our family.

We were also able to rely on our amazing neurologist at the hospital. She is a specialist in the SMA world, has a deep faith, and is the most sturdy, amazing pillar we could have ever asked for. She never forced anything on us and was an incredible partner in Lewiston's care.

* * *

It was mid-November and Lewiston's breathing became more and more of a struggle. We had been in and out of ICU. The hospice is across the street from the hospital, but every time we needed to make changes, they had to do it in the hospital. We were not authorized to just walk over, we had to call for medical transport—which was an ambulance. It was comical, and even the medical staff thought so. The drive was about forty-five meters—yes, I said METERS, that is not a typo—so, quite literally a stone's throw away into the ambulance bay, and then they would officially check him in. All a very lengthy process for what could have been a forty-second walk across the parking lot. We would have the paramedics come to the room, ask a million questions, want to strap him down to a bed (which didn't work cause he was so floppy and had no muscle tone), and then escort us down the elevator outside to the ambulance. I always insisted on holding him, so I would carry him and sit in the back seat of the ambulance for the seven seconds it took to do a U-turn and enter the ambulance bay. It was pretty silly. It took longer to do this than to walk down the stairs, across the street, and into the hospital. Sometimes, I would force the paramedics to turn on the sirens. I figured if I was in an ambulance, I might as well get the full experience.

I was so tired of these charades that I decided to take things into my own hands. Lewiston needed support in his breathing. I would think back to Hot Ronnie's dad Jimmy laying there lifeless and like a total vegetable right before he died, and I knew one thing for certain—I didn't want that for my son. But I also didn't want to just give up and throw in the towel. There were so many medical options. So many critical decisions to make. What if going on BiPAP (a breathing machine) made all the difference? What if this would drastically help him? The other thought was what if this was just a temporary solution to delay what was really coming, which was his death. Ugh, writing those words wrecks my heart and breaks it into a million pieces.

We had been fighting for a drug to try for Lewiston. I have never said this out loud, but I almost didn't want to get access to the drug for fear that it would just prolong his life and his suffering, only to drag out this crazy roller coaster called Lewiston's life before a still-too-soon death. The drug Spinraza was only being offered in two places in Canada, Vancouver and Toronto. At the time, it was still in clinical trials and not yet approved by Health Canada. We finally got approval to get treatment in Vancouver, but as Ronnie and I weighed the pros and cons, we felt it was not the best decision for our family. Lewiston could barely make it across the parking lot from the hospice house to the hospital for physio or check-ups without crashing. How would he make the flight? There was no room for me on the medical plane because it required too much equipment and medical staff. It just didn't feel right to go to Vancouver, so we trusted the nudges in our hearts and declined treatment. We got down on our knees to ask God to help us with the final decision. It was the worst feeling in the world, but we trusted our guts.

A few hours after declining the offer for Lewiston to travel to Vancouver, the drug company granted special access to us here in Calgary—right at Alberta Children's Hospital. He was the first kid in Alberta to receive this magical, life-changing drug called Spinraza. We decided not to tell any family, as we didn't want to get everyone's hopes up. He got his second treatment November 15, and then was scheduled again for his next dose on November 30. Every day was similar. Our daughter lived with us in the hospice. I would get up with her and then go and say hi to Lewiston. I would get us ready and dressed for the day. I made sure to keep showering, making my bed, and doing my hair and makeup. Those habits never died. It sounds so silly, but come what may, I needed to feel ready. I needed this simple daily habit of getting ready to keep me sane and feeling my best, all things considered.

We would wheel Lewiston back from the nurses' station and into our large family suite, and my mom would show up with a hot Starbucks mid-morning. She would bring fresh laundry and whatever else we needed from our home. We did this day in and day out. People would pop in and out through the day. We would dance and read, and sometimes I would just sit with Lewiston in the quiet. Having the many visitors helped. The nurses were like security and bouncers at times. I was thankful.

In between Spinraza treatments, Lewiston seemed to be really improving. I was even convinced that he was moving his limbs more. Things looked so good that Hot Ronnie decided to go back to work. Our life had felt like it was in total limbo, and it was surreal at times. Is our kid dying, or is this all just some sick joke? Creating some sort of normal was needed, and so Ronnie went to work. His first day back, I was scheduled to go and get my legs waxed. I, too, craved *something* normal.

That morning, everything changed. We had just finished our morning routine of bathing, dance party, oils, physio, and getting on a clean outfit for the day. But before I could change him into a sleeper, Lewiston got a plug in this throat, which meant there was mucus build-up. He didn't have the muscle strength to clear his throat, so we would suction him. Typically, we could get at it with suction or some chest physio but not this time. I was a pro at suctioning him but could not even come close to helping him. Before I knew it, he stopped breathing. He went totally limp and started turning blue. I started screaming for help—like screaming at the top of my lungs. "WHERE IS KELSEY?" is all I yelled. When the nurse Kelsey came in, which felt like forever, I screamed "This is not the end. Not like this, save him, you have to save him." I remember I was screaming at him, "Not now, please come back. You can't go, you can't go, this isn't it, please come back. Not like this."

They started on him, pumping his fragile little chest, pumping big full breaths back into this little chest. They worked on his lifeless body; I wouldn't let them stop. I just kept yelling and praying, "Not like this, please come back." I begged God. They worked on him until he was breathing again, until that plug was gone. It was one of the most horrible scenes of my life, forever etched into my mind. It is a scene I don't want to remember, a nightmare I pray no one else has to live through. I am so thankful I was the only one to witness it. Ronnie, Swayzie, and my mom were all elsewhere.

I just knew this was not how it was supposed to end. It wasn't supposed to be horrific, like a scene out of *Grey's Anatomy*. He wasn't supposed to die in chaos, but in peace—I just knew that. I will forever remember this moment when he lay there lifeless, totally still, no breath, no choking, just still. I knew this was not his time and fought so hard for them to save him. Our fiery, redhaired nurse Kelsey saved him. She didn't stop until the plug was clear and he was breathing again.

After that moment, Lewiston was never the same again.

We continued to pray, people dropped off crystals for him to sleep on, I lathered him in essential oils every day, made him swim, stretch, and do physiotherapy until I was exhausted. We still continued our daily dance parties to Justin Timberlake's song "Can't Stop the Feeling!". However, on November 21, 2016, we could tell Lewiston was done fighting, and called our pastors.

I called Jonathan and Natasha, the pastors of our church, at about 5:00 p.m., and they were at the hospice a few hours later. I held Lewiston and sat on the brown recliner with Ronnie by my side. My parents were there as we dedicated Lewiston's life to the Lord. I pictured doing this at our church, but it just didn't happen like that. I remember begging for one last miracle that night, begging God to save him.

The last hours of watching our son struggling to breathe, wondering which breath would be his last, were the most horrible. We stayed up that night watching his breaths get heavier and heavier. It was some kind of sick torture. We couldn't believe this was our life, or that this was his. It was hell on earth. I pray that no one else has to endure it.

Lewiston passed peacefully in my arms on November 22, 2016 after his morning bath. It was a long night. Ronnie and I were both exhausted. Lewiston looked up at Hot Ronnie, and it was as though he said, "Dad, I am going to be alright, but I am done fighting, and it is time to let go." He took his last breath, and just like that, his earthly body was just a body.

He passed in the morning. We brought him back from the bath to our room, and like that, it was done. Just a lifeless body wrapped up in a warm hospital blanket. It's weird. You never think about the next thing you will do after the person passes.

I texted our pastor Natasha and told her. There was peace in that for me, maybe because I felt she was a pastor and the closest thing to Heaven and a direct line with the big guy. We then called my parents to tell them. They knew it was coming, and my dad showed up within minutes of the phone call. My mom stayed with Swayzie at our house.

Our sweet Swayzie girl was such a trooper through this all. Constantly being tossed to different people, no normal routine or food. Her and my mom grew a special bond that year.

I truthfully didn't know what to do really, other than get our crap together and move on with life. And so, within an hour of him passing, we started clearing and getting our life packed up to move us back home. I wanted this chapter closed as soon as possible. We had lived in the hospice for nearly three months. We left mid-afternoon, and we decided to drive his body to the funeral home. I carried him and held him tight. We came down the elevator and at the bottom of the stairs was the entire staff from the hospice, including the chef and the cleaning staff. They stood in a semicircle and saluted us in their own way. It was one of the most moving moments of Lewiston's journey. The simple act of standing still and honouring a life. A tribute to our little lion. I was a proud mama. That day his roar was big. His legacy now even bigger. We drove his little body to the funeral home to be cremated. It was beyond weird to drop him off there. Weird to leave, weird to drive home to our house, weird, just so damn weird. I didn't even know what our next steps would be.

Lewiston changed things in that hospice. I even wrote an email a year later with all of my ideas for areas of improvement. Including hosting more dance parties. I've received notes from several members of the team saying that he reminded them to have some fun. Dealing with death is serious, but in it, you can see the beauty and joy, and yes, you can even find moments to celebrate. We saw a lot of kids pass away during our time there. I think my faith is so strong and solid because one of the greatest gifts ever given to me is grace from God and a hope in Heaven.

This is the letter that I wrote to my son on the one-year anniversary of his passing. I miss that little blue-eyed angel more than you know. If you are reading this chapter and are a mama or a dad, squeeze your little babes tighter, soak in the moments, and don't wish the moments away.

LEWISTON JAMES // To my little babe that danced into heaven way before we were ready, thank you for giving me the gift of life. Yes, little man, I am living life with all I got. Truly— you were not planned and came way earlier than we were ready for. I cried when the stick signaled you were on the way. Your sister was only four months old at the time. Little did I know, the short life you would live would be my greatest highlight and most amazing accomplishment. As quickly as you arrived, you were gone. Sometimes the biggest surprises turn out to be the biggest blessings. In losing your life, I have found mine and I believe you are helping others find theirs too. Your dad and I have deepened our marriage and I truly understand what it means to be a loving partner through good times and bad, in sickness and in health. Your handsome dad has kept us together with his unwavering faith and stubbornness. Your big sister is the light we need on tough days and is full of personality. I would have loved to see you two together. Instead, we pray patiently for God to bless us with more brothers and sisters in whichever form they come. We have started a foundation in your honour and memory. I believe your impact is reaching way beyond these Alberta borders. THANK YOU for showing us that dance brings joy regardless of how dark it is, for spreading love, and helping us choose movement instead of stagnation. We are grateful for all the memories we had. I can't wait to dance in heaven with you, but until then we will live our best life fully alive running right towards our roar. With all my love, your Mama.

THE NUDGE:

Lewiston taught me to choose movement. To move forward with joy and hope. To dance even on the darkest days. Do you feel stagnant right now? Do you feel hopeless and stuck? Follow the nudge to choose movement. Whatever that looks like for you; follow the nudge to go on a walk, to start dancing again, to start a foundation, to go back to school, to read your Bible in the mornings, write the book, ask the hot guy out, start the side hustle that will eventually turn into an empire. Just go after your goals full speed ahead. Life's too short for you to be stagnant and not move forward.

THE CHOICE:

If you aren't choosing movement, then you are choosing stagnation. Movement is about more than physical motions; it's a mindset, a way of looking at the world. You can either choose to see yourself on an incline toward a brighter and better future, or you can choose to see your life as a plateau—stagnant. What you choose to envision will determine your future. Choose movement.

THE JOY:

When you follow the nudge to get moving, you will realize your true potential. We often think we are less capable than we actually are. There is so much joy in moving beyond the limits we set on ourselves and realizing, "Oh hey, I got this. I can move forward, I'm strong enough to stand up and face life."

NOT GETTING THE MIRACLE

the nudge to accept and give grace

I'm actually pissed that God didn't give us a miracle that so many people prayed for.

It's okay, God can handle me being pissed. That miracle just wasn't in the cards for us. Some of you here today believe in God. Some of you want nothing to do with Him, and others of you believe in the parts you pick and choose that work best for you. I've been there, so I get it. The God that I believe in is a God of love. He truly is. I've questioned so many times: *how does a loving God do this to Ronnie and me? Haven't we faced enough tragedy in our life? Why would you take our sweet two-and-a-half-month-old baby boy and make him go through this? Why him?*

I asked my mom when Lewiston was first diagnosed, "What if we don't get the miracle that thousands of people are praying for?" I literally got hundreds of messages a week from people around the world saying that they were praying for us. I was so scared because what if this is the one opportunity for people to really see Jesus at work? I mean, how perfect would it be that people see this kid who was supposed to die and then he actually lives? We lived in this camp of preparing for death, but also dreaming of inviting everyone to his first little league game, which I had thought we could host at McMahon Stadium in Calgary because news outlets from around the world would want to cover it. Because every doctor and every nurse would want to witness this miracle child.

As I was asking these questions, I remember my mama said this to me, and it has stuck with me to this day:

"What if the miracle or miracles are long after he passes? What if it isn't his life that is a miracle but rather his death?

Seriously? I wanted to punch her in the face . . . how could she even think that. We needed a miracle, and we needed it now.

The day after Lewiston's funeral service, a friend of mine gave her life to Jesus. Super simple, at the kitchen table, she said she was nudged in way that she had never been nudged before. And I was mad. I said to God, "I lost my son for her? Why did an innocent baby have to die?" I struggle and wrestle with this often. I battle with the fact that my son isn't here and other people are wasting their lives. They don't care for their kids or aren't grateful for what they have.

I confessed this difficult truth to my friend Roger a few years after Lewiston's passing. We were catching up over lunch. He apologized for not being there for me. He was real and honest and cried; he could barely get the words out. I have learned that in heartache, trauma, grief, and tragedy, some people don't know how to help or show up, and that is okay. They feel awkward and out of place, so instead of running to the scene, they turn the other way. They are so scared to do the wrong thing, so they do nothing at all. They back away or back out of your life. I have learned to let go of any expectations because I truly believe that people are doing the best with what they have and with where they are at. Truth be told, it took a lot of Brené Brown to understand this shit and not be mad or hold grudges.

When I confessed my anger to Roger about the situation, about the miracles being different than the one I wanted, I told him the story about the friend getting saved and about my anger toward God that

He would sacrifice Lewiston to save her. Roger paused, he looked down at his food, a few tears fell, and then he looked right at me with watery eyes and softly said, "You ever wonder if God is saying the same thing? 'I sacrificed my son for her—for her mess. That girl who has wandered and gotten lost more times than I can count on one hand, who has promised to figure it out and keeps wasting her time, who repeatedly makes the same mistake. I keep giving her grace upon grace and she still is sorting through it.'"

I needed to hear these powerful words. God has given me so much grace, and He doesn't condemn me or regret His sacrifice to save me. His love, goodness, and grace know no bounds.

Not getting the miracle I wanted was really, really hard. And watching others get the miracle they wanted was hard too, which made me feel like a horrible person. Friends, it can be hard to hold onto faith in these seasons: when you don't get the miracle, when your prayers go unanswered, when you have more doubt than belief. In this season, I often thought back to that moment when I was twenty-one in the hospital, in that orange plastic chair, where my grandpa who was dying of cancer thanked God. He was not getting the miracle he was praying for, and still he found joy, still he found opportunities to praise and things to be grateful for. I thought of his posture in the hospital: bowing, submitting, humbling himself. His posture that day in the hospital reminds me of another Bible story.

The night before Jesus was about to die on the cross to wash away everyone's sin, he was scared shitless (I don't know if I'm allowed to say that about Jesus . . . but I mean come on, He was human and He knew He was about to die. Anyone in that situation would be scared shitless.) He went to a remote garden to pray in peace and quiet, and He said to God, "This sorrow is crushing my life out . . . My Father, if there is any way, get me out of this. But please, not what I want. You, what do you want? . . . if there is no other way than this, drinking this cup to the dregs, I'm ready. Do it your way." (Matthew 26:36-38, 39, 42 MSG).

Jesus was scared of death; He did not want to endure the pain that was before Him. But He knew that God's plan was better than His wishes. He knew that there would be more joy in God's will and plan than anyone else's plan. He knew that God loved Him and was not punishing Him; He knew that God's plan would lead to good and lead to joy. So, in this season, I wanted to mimic Jesus' posture. I wanted to humble myself, bowing low, surrendering my will and plan and expectations and disappointments, and say, "Do it your way." Man, is it hard—especially for a Type-A person like me to relinquish control over every aspect of my life. But it is so worth it.

THE NUDGE:

So often we can hold a grudge or become bitter. It is easier to do that than do the hard work of forgiveness and applying grace. But sitting in resentment will only lead to further pain. It is only through grace (receiving and giving) that we can experience the joy that life has to offer. When you are nudged to show grace (toward yourself, toward others, toward your doubts and frustrations with God) follow that nudge as far as you can.

THE CHOICE:

What if you chose grace, what if you chose faith, what if you chose to believe that people are actually doing their best (even if you think they can do better), what if you chose to not get involved and just stayed in your lane? When we don't get the miracle we are asking for, when the family member doesn't get healed, or the guy doesn't text you back (some might think this doesn't deserve to be put in the category of an unanswered prayer for a miracle, but my guess is you haven't dated in a while), or you have mountains of debt that just isn't dwindling, you have a choice. You can either drown in self-pity and resentment, or you can focus on the grace and mercy that surrounds you. The grace of waking up to a new morning with breath in your lungs, the grace of inspiring other people through your story, the grace of your little babes telling you they love you. Choose to sit and dwell on those things, choose a posture of humble submission, and watch your resentment slowly fade away.

THE JOY:

The joy comes from letting go and allowing life to continue on. Joy comes from taking another step of faith. Joy comes from understanding more of what grace is each and every day—expanding the definition and realizing that it is limitless.

LEAVE THE CHILI AT HOME

the nudge to grieve with hope

Lewiston's funeral was exactly what I wanted. I wanted twenty massive balloons lining the hallway, and my friends made sure there were TWENTY MASSIVE BALLOONS lining the hallway. I wanted food. I wanted dancing. This was a celebration of Lewiston's life and the lives that he has forever changed.

I also wanted people to see that in all of the tragedy, we could still give praise and thanks to a good and loving God, just like my grandpa did when life seemed awfully dark and scary. So, there was crying, dancing, laughing, and reflecting. It was a perfect tribute. It was a perfect picture of the depth of joy and emotion that Lewiston brought to our lives.

* * *

A few days after Lewiston's funeral, Hot Ronnie and I got on a plane to Hawaii. I was so sick of making medical decisions, organizing funeral arrangements, and having people check in and drop off yet *another* pot of chili. I wanted to be alone and for no one to be able to come and visit us. I needed space. I had dreamed of going to Hawaii forever but with different circumstances. We left our daughter at home with my mom and my mother-in-law. It was hard to do, but I needed to just focus on me and Ronnie for a couple of days. We had sex again, we hugged, we read books, we chilled, we swam, we explored, we held hands and strolled the beach. Hot Ronnie made sure we worked out every day. We adventured and ate really good overpriced food. And you know what? We even laughed. We drank fancy cocktails and took some much-needed time to just be.

One night, we ended up eating at the bar of the restaurant Monkey Pod in Maui. Hot Ronnie hates sitting at the bar because you have to make small talk with the people sitting beside you. We sat down, and within seconds, the guy beside us starts chatting up a storm.

"What brings you here to Hawaii?" he asked

"Need a break from the city." Hot Ronnie responded.

"Oh yeah, I know that feeling. You got kids?" he asked.

"Yep."

"How many kids do you have? How old are they?"

And then there it was. This question is one of the toughest questions that grieving parents have to face. Do you lie? Do you just blurt out the truth to a total stranger that your six-month-old son passed away one week ago and you're here trying to catch your breath again? It was the first time we had to answer a question like that. As bereaved parents, this will always be our struggle. Questions like, "How many kids do you have, how old?" or "Where is your other child?" It is so hard for strangers to understand why one of the kids is not with us.

I don't mind talking about Lewiston. In fact, I love it. My friend always says, "When we stop saying their name, that is when our little ones truly die." I don't want Lewiston's name to ever die. And so, I talk about him as much as I can. If people ask, I am happy to chat about it.

But what I do mind is when people stop looking at you in the face and get awkward when you say your child is dead or has passed away. It's like, dude we are all going to die. We are all going to hit some heartache and lose somebody. So, chill out. I have read a lot of Brené Brown books to deal with vulnerability and some of these emotions. In several of her books, she talks about what happens when we believe that others are doing the best that they can with what they have. This was a mind-blowing perspective for me, as it took off a bunch of guilt I was placing on others. I was mad at certain friends for, in my opinion, the shitty job they were doing at walking along side us during Lewiston's fight and his death.

I learned a lot about grief during this time. A lot about coping and what's helpful and what's not. Everybody's ways of coping are different, but I want to share a little of my process, in case it brings comfort to even one person.

HOW I COPED FOR THE FIRST FEW WEEKS

When Lewiston died, I went to the mall and spent a lot of money. We had a GoFundMe set up for us to help us because I wasn't able to go back to work when Lewiston was born. I had no maternity leave or funds coming in. Ronnie's business partners were great and very understanding and beyond generous to us. The GoFundMe money was used for all sorts of medical expenses, funeral costs—Holy Lord, are funerals expensive—and all the things in between. We were even able to bless some less fortunate families that were struggling as well. And yes, I took some of that money and went into my favourite shoe store, Stuart Weitzman, and bought three new pairs of shoes. Yep three! (Two of which don't fit anymore cause of my third pregnancy, but at the time they were unreal). The shoes were all on sale, so I justified it. I then got a whole new wardrobe at Aritzia, thinking that it would make me feel better. It did for a few days. It was nice to reach for a few items that made me feel put together, but I soon found out that shopping and spending money doesn't make grief go away. (Well, I bought a few more things before I really learned that lesson.)

I spent money getting Swayzie's playroom just right and bought Hot Ronnie a TV since up until then we only owned one. I wanted to create a sweet man cave for him to watch football in, thinking this would help him in his grief. If we just had a great space for Swayzie, if Ronnie had the perfect set up for Sunday Football, if I had beautiful shoes and nice clothes, we would be able to get over this faster. I spent money to bring things into our life to make it feel more complete or more full. Buying things I had wanted for a long time, like the playroom items and TV, made me feel like we were moving forward. This was just a superficial way of feeling like we were fine—like putting a Band-Aid over a bullet hole. It helps for a brief second, but the bleeding is so deep that the Band-Aid can only hold for so long.

Ronnie and I handled the grief very differently, yet at the same time, pretty similarly. To be honest, losing a kid is messed up, and apparently the divorce rates sky rocket when you deal with loss and tragedy like this. I get it. It takes a lot of work to not want to rip each other's heads off.

Grief is real. It comes in waves just like they say it does. I don't cry a lot. I actually went to see a therapist in the first year and said that I was worried that I didn't cry more. I rarely cried—it was weird. I think I had built up a barrier to ensure I never got too weak or low, and that meant I rarely cried because that felt weak. I was really hurting the second Christmas Lewiston should have been with us; we barely mentioned his name. That hurt and emotion caused a massive blow-up with my family. When that fight broke out, it was like the floodgates opened up.

My dad, who is the gruff, non-emotional farmer that says he loves me only about two or three times a year, confessed while choking back tears that he didn't like talking about Lewiston because it was "just too hard." You see, my parents were there for the death and the darkness, and my dad was the first to show up moments after he passed. Literally minutes after I called him, he was there trying to pick up the pieces to help take away the pain, the loss, the sting. He started cleaning and sorting and collecting our life in the hospice minutes after Lewiston took his last breath because he knew he couldn't physically take away the pain, but he could help me by doing these practical tasks. I didn't know how to function or the right way to handle the grief and loss. And so we cleaned and organized because that is what I needed, and it was the only thing either of us knew to do.

My mom confessed that losing a grandchild is like a double loss. You not only lose a grandchild, but you are watching your own child suffer through the loss. My mom came to the hospice every day to look after Swayzie, do the laundry, get us meals, bring hot coffees, and sit with me. Just being there as a support system.

I think that the hardest part about grief is not knowing how long it will last. I mean, grief is forever. I will never stop grieving my son. But how long does it hurt, how long does it feel like we are going to be suffocating for? How long will it feel dark? Here is what I know: grief is a mother F'er. It can take you down or you can show it who is boss.

***

In spring, Hot Ronnie and I joined family grief counselling through the Alberta Children's Hospital. There were about ten other families besides ours. Man oh man was that hard. In one of the sessions, you go around the circle and talk about your child, say their name, and tell how they passed. TALK ABOUT BRUTAL. It went something like this:

"Hey, my name is Jess, and my son passed away just shy of his six-month birthday. He had SMA, a rare genetic disease that we had no clue that we were carriers of."

The room was filled with lots of tears and so much heartache and sadness. But it also gave us perspective. Ronnie and I had the gift of knowing our son was dying, we got to make amazing memories and say goodbye. It wasn't unexpected or sudden. I felt we had time to prepare. So many people's children were killed instantly; they had no warning. One moment here, and the next gone, be it cancer, car accidents, drowning incidents. I remember thanking God that day that we knew Lewiston was at the end because, as terrible as it was, it gave us time to say goodbye and really come to peace with letting him go. As much as you can come to peace with your kid's death.

My peace comes when I think about how Lewiston is now whole and complete and healthy. The other day, Swayzie asked about heaven and Lewiston, and it made me smile. It made my heart swell with pride that I can say that we believe in a good God who made a way for us to get to heaven. It isn't about works or deeds or certain rules but simply grace and believing with your whole heart that God is God. And that He wants us there with Him. We told Swayzie that there is no more pain or suffering, and that it has the most beautiful gardens you have ever seen. This is not just a story to make my four-year-old feel better. It is truly what I believe. The picture that I cling to is Ronnie's dad Jimmy and Lewiston playing baseball, eating hotdogs, running around and laughing together, soaking in the sunshine.

Our grief journey hasn't been easy. I have gone to therapy like I mentioned, and have done what I could to stay healthy. I got anxiety, but it didn't come out the way I thought it would. For me, my anxiety presented itself in rage and anger—severe rage and anger. I would just lose it on Ronnie. Let me give you an example of what I mean by rage and anger. It all started out with a rice maker, yes, a rice maker. Ronnie had used the rice maker for our new restaurant concept, HULA—a franchise store that makes the best Poke bowls in town. Ronnie was doing recipe testing, and it looked like nineteen batches of rice had been made in it. Because nineteen batches of rice *had* been made in it. Hot Ronnie was working on menu items for the restaurant. The day was long and busy, so he never got around to cleaning it. The rice was hard and caked into the pot and all over the lid. It looked like it had not been cleaned in three years. And so, when Ronnie brought it back home, I lost it. I mean I was swearing and firing off F bombs like I had never fired off before. I even mentioned divorce. Who threatens to divorce someone over a dirty rice maker? That is how my pain, my grief, my hurt would show up. I would think I was totally fine, and then boom, something that didn't go the way I wanted would make me rage in all sorts of ways. Even rice.

Another example of my hulk-like rage happened when the barista at Starbucks told me my cinnamon dolce sprinkles were going to cost fifty cents, and I had never paid for them in my life. I wanted to punch her and yell and write an email to her boss, to the CEO of the entire Starbucks Corporation, to Mr. Starbucks himself. My son died; can you not spare the dang cinnamon dolce sprinkles you jerk? It also really pisses me off when there is not consistency from one store to the next. In my grief and anxiety, my temper gets short, like really short, and I take it out on the people I love the most—my hubby and kids and coffee providers. My kids will be kids and not listen about putting on a coat. We will be rushing to get out the door and because we are late and every second counts, and I just lose it. So much rage forms up in me, I feel like fire is coming out of my nostrils.

Grief will snag you at the most unexpected time. For me, it pops up when things aren't in my control. I need a sense of order and calm, but I also need all cylinders functioning at top speed. So, when my iPhone decides to stop working, I lose it. I remember being in the Apple store, and when the Apple employee was trying to help me and I felt like they were not getting it, I just started bawling. There it was: grief showing up when you least want it to, when you are not prepared, when you're with strangers and no one understands why some blonde chick is bawling her eyes out over her silly iPhone. Experiencing these feelings has taught me a lot about empathy and compassion. You just never know what someone is going through. Remember this the next time you see a blonde chick crying at an Apple store, in a Starbucks, or in an airport bathroom.

I don't think there is a secret sauce for grief or a right or a wrong way to do it. No judgment here. You do you! But what I do know is true is that grief shouldn't isolate you, and you shouldn't hide from it. Not feeling the emotions or pretending something didn't happen is a recipe for a disaster and another blow up. Find community, reach out for help, embrace the suck, work through the emotions. Don't let anger control your life or cripple you from living life to the fullest, and find healing. When you lose someone, the grief will never just go away. So, choose to work through it.

Here is the short list of things that helped me:

1. Talking to a professional, a counselor or therapist. Don't be stubborn, just book a damn appointment.

2. Being totally honest with my feelings.

3. Planning regular dates with close friends to fill me up. Often

this would involve getting sweaty together at a fitness class, but one of my favourite times with my friends was a trip to LA.

4. Working out. It literally changes the chemistry in your brain. Hence why it changes your mindset. As Rachel Hollis says, "Move your body, change your mind."

5. Eating right. We need proper fuel to fight for a good life, so put in the best damn fuel you can find. Cookies, a tub of ice cream, a bag of chips . . . sister, those ain't going to bring back Lewiston from the dead; those are only going to put on extra pounds on my hips.

6. Showering and making my bed every day. Sounds super simple, but it is harder than you think when you're in the depths of grief. Get up and get your butt in the shower, do your hair and makeup, and put on real clothes. There haven't been any real days where I have just stayed in bed all day and watched Netflix and kept the curtains drawn, the room dark and just not moved. I had a little girl that got me out of bed, and what a blessing that was. I knew if I went down that hole of allowing myself to go dark and stay stagnant, I might never come up or get out. Yes, it is way easier to stay in darkness than it is to find the light. Staying in the dark is easy because you simply just don't move. I had to move to find the light, to find new breath. I know the triggers that send me down the dark hole, and I will do everything in my power to avoid those. You see, I believe with my whole heart that some days when the darkness is all around, I needed to be the light and bring the light.

7. Traveling and adventure. Try something new, a new city, a new activity, just step out of your comfort zone and do it.

So many people ask me how I do this, how I keep going even in grief. I don't really have a magic formula or secret mantra that I repeat. I just have had those gentle nudges telling me that life is meant to be lived—lived to the fullest with purpose. Your days are numbered, and spending them in bed isn't going to change a damn thing. You get a choice, girlfriend. You get a damn choice on how your life gets to look. So, get up, shower, put on a great outfit, grab some mascara, and get moving.

NAVIGATING GRIEF & HELPING FAMILIES WALK THROUGH TRAUMA AND ILLNESS

I get asked a lot of questions about how to help a family in need. People want to know what is the best way to help, how we navigated it, how we managed, and if I have any tips. So, I made a simple list. Let's start with the things NOT to do:

Things NOT to do:

1. When visiting someone in the hospital who is sick or terminally ill, the best visit is a short visit. Read that again. THE BEST VISIT IS A SHORT VISIT. Don't wait for them to ask you to leave. It's not the person's job to entertain you. Far too often, people would visit because it made them feel better. Don't be stupid. Get in and get out, unless they ask you to stay longer.

2. When taking pictures, if you get permission to do so, don't fix your hair and make sure you look perfect. This is called grief tourism. If you need to post it, post it and stop worrying about looking just so. Ensure the visit wasn't just about showing the whole world that you went and visited the sick kid in the hospital.

3. Don't say stupid stuff. If you don't know if it is appropriate, don't say it at all. Examples of horrible things people have said to me (I kid you not):

   - *"I know exactly how you feel, my cat just passed away two months ago and was like family. He was my first baby."* No, no you don't know what I went through—you did not conceive your cat, then grow it for nine months and birth your cat out of your vagina—sorry to my cat-loving friends, but a cat's death is NOT the same as the death of a child.

   - *"Don't worry, you will get over it."* Excuse me while I barf and try not to punch you in the face.

   - *"Your grief isn't as bad as mine was. I knew my son for longer; he was fourteen when he passed away."* Grief is grief—enough said. WE NEVER COMPARE GRIEF!

   - *"My friend lost her cousin a few years ago."* Why are you telling me this? It isn't relevant. I don't know your cousin, that doesn't help me at all, so just don't say it.

- *"You're lucky you're so strong. It gives you a real advantage."* Advantage? No ma'am, I just choose not to let sorrow swallow me whole. And it's a fight every single day.

4. If you offer to do something, do it. Don't bail. Don't say you will come shovel the side walk or bring freshly cut up veggies if you are not going to follow through.

Helpful things you can do:

1. Make a meal, but for the love of God, **leave the chili at home**. The people that wanted to really show up for us made gourmet meals. They made different courses and made us feel loved by their thoughtfulness. Anyone can do chili, and trust me, five other people have already brought it, so get creative. Not a cook? Find the best restaurant, explain the situation, and demand that they do take out. Bring them containers if you must, or ask a friend who is a gourmet chef to help. Chances are damn good they will be over the moon to use their skills to bless a family in need. If you don't have the time to do it, then don't.

2. Bake a fresh batch of muffins and bring them over straight out of the oven. Remember a short visit is the best visit, or drop them off with a little note.

3. Get a gift card for Skip the Dishes, a meal delivery service like Uber Eats, or a gift card to their favourite restaurant. Skip and

Uber were not around yet, but we have since sent it to friends that are in other cities where we physically can't get to.

4. Show up and do yard work, shovel their sidewalk if it snows, cut the grass, clean their gutters, water the lawn or plants. Don't ask, just do it. In a time of grief, you often can't stand to make one more decision. So, don't make someone make another silly decision. Get creative and just simply figure it out. *"I will come by Tuesday at 5:00 p.m. to cut your grass."*

5. Babysit if they have more than one kid. Take their kids out for a play date or to a movie, just give them a break.

6. Send them a house cleaner. It might stretch your budget, but I can guarantee you that a year from now, you won't miss the $150 that you spent on it. Your financial mess will more likely be from a repeated bad use of money like too many shoes and trips to Sephora where all you needed was mascara but snagged a basket full of products you don't even use. Grab a few friends and have everyone chip in to help clean your friend's home.

7. In the months after death, pick up the phone and call. Send a text related to the situation. I had one friend text me on the twenty-fifth of each month for two years straight to say she was thinking about me and Lewiston. Didn't cost her a cent. What it did cost was her time, and sometimes that is all I needed.

* * *

I want to share this last story of how people showed up. There are so many—I wish I had done a better job of documenting it, but I was living minute to minute and just trying to keep my kids alive and soak in the moments. If you showed up for our family in any way, I am sorry you never got a thank you card. I hope you didn't expect one. But please know your acts of thoughtfulness and kindess is what kept our family upright. Me especially, as acts of service is my love language. I had become friends with a girl who took my spin class. I bought her a coffee once after my class as a thank you for being regular. I had no idea that that gesture would lead to one of the most meaningful and special relationships.

She constantly showed up at the hospital—green juice, salad, Americano, you name it. Never overstayed her welcome just showed up when my tank was low. *Oh you're exhausted, lonely, and need a shoulder to cry on—let me bring a bottle of chilled white wine and my famous popcorn.* She would sit with me in the darkness—late at night when the halls were dim and only the sounds of machines beeping could be heard. She would sit with me and be a shoulder to cry on, and even now, almost four years after Lewiston's death, she sits with me.

I was struggling with my mental health after our third child was born, and Hot Ronnie knew that no matter how many pep talks he gave me, I needed it from my bestie. We sat in the stillness of a summer evening and she gave me a swift kick in the ass and told me she believed in me. "There's nobody I believe in more than you, Janzen. So, stop beating yourself up that it hasn't come quicker and keep going. Oh, and just remember all the good you have spread and lives you have changed." Be that friend. Show up when the buzz of being the "it" family to help has worn off; stay in their corner and keep dropping off the hot coffees and green jucies because the reality is that the pain doesn't just disappear after two months of grieving.

* * *

Even still, even with all the dos and don'ts and therapy and taming the rage, the lies will creep in. And these lies will make you feel like you can't move and are basically stuck in quicksand. This happened to me often in the first two years after Lewiston passed. I would sit at my desk with every intention to work and write this book, and then three hours would go by and not a thing would get accomplished. Not one thing, except for exercising my thumb on Instagram. I would wonder why I wasn't more productive. I would try to get started on stuff but just wasn't able to make any progress. I would tell myself that I was useless, not worthy, stupid, and my ideas were outrageous. I actually began to believe this because I couldn't move the needle even just an inch. Procrastination was my drug of choice.

I had to ask for help. It got so bad that the lies would paralyze me. I would start to spiral down a deep, dark hole. I knew my grief and anxiety were getting worse and worse, so I knew I needed a game plan to fix this or things would go sideways pretty quick. I figured out a way to deal with it. I called a friend and told her what I was walking through and how ugly and dark it really was. She didn't judge me for a second and was willing to come along side me. I would say, "It's dark, and the lies are creeping in." And she would start speaking truth to me. She would tell me the beautiful truth that I was not useless, I was worthy and had purpose, and I was smart and able.

I would then stand in my bathroom mirror and repeat those things to myself, sometime with her still on the phone. Yes, I would stand in my bathroom, face the mirror, and tell myself I was able. I was powerful. I

195

could focus. I was worthy. My ideas had meaning. I had purpose.

Maybe, just maybe, you need someone else to tell you it will be okay.

Trust me. It is going to be okay. More than okay. Why?

Because you get to make it okay. You get that choice. I am living proof that it works.

THE NUDGE:

Grief can feel so heavy. Though it never completely goes away, it gets easier to carry—especially when you follow nudges to let people help you carry your grief. Don't close yourself out, don't hide. Find ways to cope. Don't stay stuck. Let the light in.

THE CHOICE:

Choosing to grieve with hope is a really hard uphill battle. Choosing to be vulnerable and let people in when you're grieving is kind of a shit show, but it is so worth it. You can choose to be prideful and take care of everything on your own when shit hits the fan, or you can let people into the mess, the grief, the hardship and let them help you. Accepting gifts, love, and support from people is really hard for me, but when I realized that there was absolutely no way that Ronnie and I could do this in our own strength, with our own resources, I chose to open my hands and open my heart.

THE JOY:

Joyful grieving sounds like an oxymoron. But I swear, it is possible. Happy grieving might be an oxymoron, but steadfast, lasting, grounding joy—that, my friends, sticks with you in all seasons, even seasons of grief. The joy of grieving with hope comes in sporadic bursts at first, and then it comes more frequently. When you choose to let light into the darkness, it might feel wrong at first (why am I dancing at my son's funeral?) but with it comes amazing joy, contagious joy.

LOVE FOR LEWISTON

the nudge to dance even in darkness

To be honest, 2017 was such a blur.

I recently heard a podcast in which the host was talking about slowing down, and that many of us don't want to actually slow down because then we're forced to face our pain. In that first year of Lewiston passing, I lived large and fast. You could say I was numbing the pain.

I didn't necessarily want to slow down and process all that had happened to me since we entered that hospital months ago, but when I was finally able to pause and reflect, I really defined my purpose. I knew that I was meant to be a light for those stuck in darkness. I wanted to bring others joy and show them that joy was possible, even in and after death. I learned to accept our story, and it pushed me to continue to be brave. I did all of the things that I could do. I went to therapy, worked out, and journaled.

It was March 2017, four months after Lewiston had gone up to heaven, and a few friends started asking about what we want to do for Lewiston's first birthday party. The last thing I wanted to do was sit at home and mope, so I sent a text message to my friends and said if anyone wanted to help plan Lewiston's birthday, come to my place on Monday night at 7:00 p.m.

Everyone I sent the text message to showed up to brainstorm.

We threw out a hundred ideas and ultimately landed on a fundraiser for the Alberta Children's Hospital Foundation with a live and silent auction. I thought it would be a brilliant idea to auction off Hot Ronnie and some friends in speedos. We planned that party in seven weeks. All I wanted to do was sell out and raise $10,000 for the hospital and hospice that Lewiston passed away in. I looked back on my notes and had written: "Our goal is to raise $10,000. Holy shit, maybe we can even raise $15,000."

We sold out the day before the event. I asked for big favors from friends and business owners and pushed hard. I literally talked to everyone I could find. Funny story, all the stress of the party made me have a massive blow up. I threw trays of cookies everywhere and must have looked like a total spaz. I actually looked like a five-year-old who didn't get what they asked for at Christmas. Someone had mixed up the gluten-free cookies with the regular cookies. That was truly the only issue we had that day. But, understandably, my stress levels were high.

The evening started, and no one but me really knew about the cookie mix up. The party could not have gone any better. We auctioned off friends and awesome prizes, and then to close out the night, we sang happy birthday to Lewiston and shot off confetti cannons. It could not have gone any better. It was beyond epic. We ended up raising over $42,000, well beyond the goal of $10,000.

So, I figured, why stop there? I felt nudged to raise $100,000 by the end of the year. And so, we began driving hard for the $100,000. We announced it again on my social media and did all of the things. We officially formed the Love for Lewiston Foundation. We started out with this idea to start a foundation, something simple to help raise money for the hospital, but also something to help the families fighting SMA and their medical needs. We also dreamed of funding critical research.

The foundation has been a labor of love. We had no clue what we were doing—not one. single. clue. I had never run a board meeting or had to make critical decisions on large amounts of money. It has been like drinking from a fire hose. But day by day, nudge by nudge, we figured it out. With our mission to create awareness about Spinal Muscular Atrophy and raise funds to find a cure for SMA at the core of every endeavor, we have been able to make a big impact through Love for Lewiston. We have been able to host incredible parties, golf tournaments, and movement events to move toward our goal. That dream I had to become a CEO? I feel like it came true after all, albeit in a very different way than I could have ever imagined.

In June 2017, Health Canada approved the first ever treatment called Spinraza for those fighting SMA. It has been a long battle to actually get access, and if Lewiston was born in 2019, it would be a totally different story.

* * *

In 2017, we reached our $100,000 goal, and Love for Lewiston has cumulatively raised over $700,000 since it started. By the end of 2020, we will have raised a total of one million dollars, Lord willing. Those funds have been used to provide countless wheelchairs for those diagnosed with SMA, renovate the hospice center where Lewiston spent his last few months, fund critical research for SMA, and fund critical needs at Alberta Children's Hospital.

Our motto at Love for Lewiston is: *Choose Movement. Bring Joy. Spread Love.* We fight for people with SMA to have more days and more dance parties. We fight for a higher quality of life for those diagnosed. We fight for families who are in the hospital to feel more at home there. We fight so that they can access care, physio, and other unconventional treatments. We fight to take the financial strain off a family, because even though we think we have free healthcare up here in Canada, nothing is ever really free. We fight to bring light to the darkness. In thinking of Lewiston's life, you can't help but think of dance parties, the joys that his smile brought, and the love that encircles him through the amazing community around him. That's why we do what we do; that's why we run this organization. For him, for his legacy.

THE NUDGE:

Often times, when you go through trauma or a season of struggle, other people around you have gone through something similar. We often feel so alone in our grief. While it is true that no one knows exactly how you feel because we all have different personalities, memories, capacities, etc., in actuality, there are people all around you who are walking through what you just walked through. Maybe they are two steps behind you, maybe twenty, maybe a hundred. Regardless, you have the chance to speak life, wisdom, guidance, and hope into their circumstances by the way you carry yourself through life. It's okay if you throw a few cookie platters in the process, but embracing celebration and opening yourself up to dream again—fueled by a renewed sense of purpose—really is a beautiful gift.

THE CHOICE:

You have the choice to wallow and sit in your trauma and pain, or you can process it with people in a healthy way. Go to a therapist, write it out, find a way to express your emotions. Then share what you learned along your journey. You are equipped and prepared to help others bring more joy and hope to their painful circumstances.

THE JOY:

When you see an opportunity to encourage others who are going through something you've gone through, take it. Blessing others with the resources, finances, encouragement, and support they need is the most beautiful thing that I've seen come out of trauma.

EASY AS PLATZ

the nudge to water the grass where you are

Remember that moment in the hospital with my grandparents? At the beginning of the book, in the orange plastic chair?

I thought about that moment often when we were in the hospital with Lewiston. I remember one day in the hospital, it was just me, Ronnie, and Lewiston in the room. There was a quietness and a peace that rested over us. I remember sitting in the corner of the hospital room as Lewiston slept, and I thought back to the day I visited my grandpa in the hospital. The chair I was in at that moment was multiple shades of brown and very cushiony, but Cushiony Brownish Chair doesn't make a good chapter title. I thought about that bright orange plastic chair, I thought about the smuggled-in piece of platz, I thought about the remarkable display of love that I was able to witness that day. And now, years later, there was a new depth to that moment I witnessed between my grandparents. I was now able to more fully realize the tenderness and pain that moment carried, along with the history, commitment, and deep joy—all mixed in. I looked over at Hot Ronnie and knew that in him, I had found what I was looking for all those years ago.

I'm so thankful for everyone who supported us during this season, but I truly could have not done it without him—my partner and teammate. I know that trauma like this can destroy marriages and pull people apart, but I'm thankful that wasn't the case with me and Hot Ronnie. God truly provided for and protected us during this time. And we fought, oh we fought, to remain close and connected. It was so hard. Even while living at the hospital, not getting nearly enough sleep, dealing with the stress of finances, grieving in different ways and at different times—through all of it, we fought to remain close.

Ronnie is my rock; he points me back to Jesus, he carries me when I'm too weak to stand on my own, he encourages me like no other. He loves me unconditionally and unwaveringly. Even in times of pain and hardship, he brings joy and tenderness to every moment.

There are still days I want to rip his head off, like why can't he just take out the trash AND replace the garbage bag so it is ready to go like I do? Or why can't he just fully clean up the kitchen, like take the food bits out of the drain of the sink and put them in the compost? He always leaves a few things undone, like one or two glasses in the sink. He doesn't pull the sheet super tight and crisp when making the bed like I do, nor does he fold the laundry how I would. All of this stuff drives me crazy. Some of it is maddening for me.

But what is more maddening for me than a few dirty dishes among the mostly clean ones is when people just stop trying to clean up any mess and throw in the towel. I have seen it time and time again. It gets hard and you stop investing in your partner, so they stop investing in you. You are more worried about keeping up with the Joneses than you are about deepening your marriage and family life. You go so fast you forget to include your partner in the dream, and all the crazy racing around to kids' activities and making sure the house stays together becomes so consuming that you forget the vision and commitment you made to one another on your wedding day. It is so easy to throw around the Big D word. Trust me, I have done it way too many times. "Fine, then let's just get a DIVORCE."

Spoiler alert: we did not get divorced. Instead, we took some time to invest in our marriage (more like I forced us to). I had just finished reading *Girl, Wash Your Face* by Rachel Hollis. I had seen so many people post about this book with this chick on the front cover getting sprayed by a fire hydrant. I had to read it. I crushed the book in about a week, and then started listening to Rachel and her husband Dave's podcasts. About a year and half after I started Love for Lewiston, I impulse-bought tickets for a marriage conference hosted by Rachel and Dave after they were promoting it on their podcast episode.

"Swayzie, tell Daddy that we have a surprise for him. Tell him we are going on a special trip."

Hot Ronnie could hear me telling Swayzie this. He later told me he thought I was surprising him with a sporting event, but in all reality, I was surprising him with this marriage conference.

Ronnie was pissed that I spent money we didn't have—he had every right to be, given the fact I put our business account into overdraft to make this trip happen. Not something I recommend, but I was desperate to go. Ronnie was mad at me for not only the stupid financial decision but booking something on a whim. But the morning we left, he changed his attitude around and told me he would go all in. And that he did. The conference was called Rise Together, and it was put on by Rachel and Dave and the Hollis Co.

I loved Rachel's book, and I was hopeful the conference would be impactful for both me and Ronnie. If anything, I figured we would hear some encouragement and walk away energized to work on our marriage. Turns out, this trip was so important for our relationship. We had been in survival mode for such a long time, and it was time to face some conversations we had been avoiding. One of my favourite things Rachel said at the conference was, "The grass is greenest where you water it." This saying has been said hundreds of time before I heard her say it, but it was this time that it stuck. I was done wishing our marriage was something it was not, while doing nothing to change it. I took a bold risk to get us there; I trusted my nudge, and man, did it pay off. I wanted to water the grass I was standing on, not wish that it would someday be better. Creating a great marriage takes work—and a lot of it.

Our marriage has grown leaps and bounds because of this conference. We communicate better and are more passionate and totally aligned. We know how to better grow together and support one another. But with the conference came some major truth bombs.

I confessed to Hot Ronnie that I had gotten lip injections—they were so subtle that not even he noticed. He was mad I hadn't been honest, and he told me I was beautiful and didn't need to do any of that. I had wanted to see what it was like more so out of curiosity than anything. And for the record because one of you is going to ask, yes, I still get them done and love it. It's so natural you can't even tell. We laughed about it, and then it came his turn for a confession—this one was a lot heavier than lip injections.

"I hate that we have the Love for Lewiston foundation," he said.

This comment broke my heart. But it made sense. It caused a lot of stress and grief in our life. I loved our foundation. It had done so much good and was truly making a difference. However, the truth of the matter was that we wouldn't need a foundation if our son was still living, we wouldn't be pouring everything we had into Love for Lewiston if Lewiston was still here. The foundation was hurting us financially because I never did return back to work after Lewiston passed. I spent all of my time volunteering, going to events, building relationships with potential donors and networking, which meant spending less time with my family. Hot Ronnie always picked up the pieces and kept the groceries stocked, the laundry up to date, the floors vacuumed, and made sure Swayzie had fun activities planned. I was running ragged, and he constantly picked up the pieces to keep us afloat. In front of everyone we looked amazing, but behind the scenes was exhausting and majorly wearing on our marriage.

As a note, we have since made some changes so that our foundation does not cause anger but great joy for our family. I have put in better boundaries and learned to ask for help. We have an army of friends that volunteer countless hours. Friends that show up, follow through and give to this foundation like it is one of our children. If you are part of this army, you know exactly who you are—THANK YOU! Words will never be enough. It isn't always easy, but in the end, we so strongly believe in the work that we are doing. We are working on a rhythm that works best for our family. I am not sure about this whole balance thing—I picture life like a teeter-totter: it is almost near impossible to keep it completely level. What I am sure of is that there are seasons of life. It ebbs and flows. What I am also sure of is that the grass is always greener where you water it.

I highly recommend that if you are married, no matter where you are at—invest in your marriage. Go away for the weekend, stay in a hotel in your own city just to get away, go on regular date nights, and book a conference together. The conference truly was a game-changer for us and helped us pause to work through stuff. It is rare that couples sit down and actually work through stuff that they really need to work on without the distractions of everyday business getting in the way. The thing is, life is happening all around us, and often we are scared to ask it to pause while we get ourselves sorted.

Ronnie and I laughed about how things have only gone uphill from there, especially in the last few years. We stopped and took note and inventory of where things were between us and then really dug in. To be honest, I thought I was a great partner, but in hindsight, I was below average. If you are struggling in your marriage, I encourage you to take inventory, take stock of what is happening. Are you treating your partner the way you want to be treated? Have you planned a special date night, have you given it everything you've got? Or have you gotten lazy, closed off, and turned to Netflix and girls nights to numb the pain? Stop booking bitch nights with your girlfriends and pour a night into your hubby. Book tickets to a sporting event and spend that energy on your partner.

Marriage is going to be unfair; you have to be selfless. Stop focusing on yourself and start focusing on how you can serve your partner. Maybe that sounds backward, but trust me. Test this theory for three months, and I guarantee your marriage will look a lot different. If both parties always put the other first, there is enough love to go around. Try this: show up how you want to be shown up for. Now before you send me hate mail saying "how can I serve my partner if I don't take care of myself blah blah blah," just try it—try just going all in. Try just showing up with no expectations other than how can you best serve your partner and watch the romance and magic unfold.

For so long, Hot Ronnie had asked me to be on his team, and I didn't get it. I didn't fully understand what it meant to be a true partner. I always had to be right and "win" the argument. No idea why I was so stubborn about always being right when he was just asking me to be a team member. (Anybody remember JJ Hammer? That girl might have still been in me . . .) I now picture going into a battlefield, and my ride-or-die is Hot Ronnie for life. Does he drive me crazy? Um, yep. Does he load the dishwasher incorrectly? All the dang time! Does he make the bed just so and straighten the sheets the way I like? Not even close. Does he clean as deeply as I do?

Nope. But he loves me and he loves me good, and the man is the most incredible father any kid could ask for. I have seen him time and time again stand up for me, defend me, and go above and beyond to ensure my safety, my care, and my health.

And just as I've told you, a vision to see things differently is so crucial to seeing joy in our circumstances. All too often, we focus on all the crap and forget to see the goodness. Sure, I could make a long list of all the shitty things in my life. Or, I can make a list of all the joy and goodness in my life. If you are struggling, I would encourage you right now to make a list. Stop reading this book right now. Seriously, stop. These words will still be here—write down your list. Write inside the dang book if you can't find paper. Write down the things in your life that bring you joy. Turn on some mellow music and write until your hand has a cramp in it from writing for so long. Because I know this: Life is good if you choose to see the goodness, the greatness, the joy, the light! Friends, LET THE LIGHT IN!

For me my list starts with drinking hot French press coffee in the morning in my favourite mug, great sex with my husband, having a comfy bed to sleep in, summer trips that include wake surfing and evening boat rides with the best of friends. It looks like swimming and sun tanning and jumping off docks, and traveling in airplanes to new cities to explore. My favourite shoes, a comfy sweatshirt or hoodie, or putting on heels and grabbing dinner with friends. All of these are what I think of as Joy Starters—especially the hot coffee and waking up early in the morning. Create a day in which you have Joy Starters—mine always includes hot coffee, a shower, and making my damn bed. I mean, to be honest, I am working on this celery juice thing, but folks, we are not quite there yet. Some of my other Joy Starters are a morning workout and journaling to get my head and heart right. Thank you Rachel Hollis and Hollis Co for the Start Today Journal.

I am on my third one as I write this book, and it has changed my life. Truly. I have bought over fourteen journals and gifted them to friends when I feel nudged to give because I believe it can change their life like it did mine. Focusing on gratitude and the dreams you have is key in bringing the joy.

So many people ask us how Ronnie and I did any of this, and time and time again, I come back to our faith. We both have a solid faith and are on the same page. If you have read this far, you know that my belief in God is no secret. I think we complicate a lot of things. I think people are scared to go all in and say out loud that they believe in Jesus, the Father, and the Holy Spirit. I still am nervous to do that to this very day—sometimes in certain groups or on social media, I wonder what people will think of me. The fear of rejection, not being included or whatever it may be. Claiming your faith can be scary, but what I believe is even more scary is believing this life is all there is. Without our hope in heaven, there is *no way* I would be okay. There is no way our marriage would be okay. Picture sitting in a hospice. Picture your own child. Now you are sitting in a big lazy boy chair waiting for him to take his last breath, every breath is harder and harder to take. He is pale and looks lifeless. He looks weak and oh so tired. He takes his last breath and then there you are holding him dead in your arms.

Trust me, you are gonna want to believe in heaven.

You see, when I lost Lewiston, I knew it was just his earthly body that would be gone. I know it is just a matter of time before I meet him again up in heaven. Disease free, pain free, he no longer suffers or struggles to breathe; he is now whole and perfect. I believe he will come running at me and greet me with the strongest, most solid embrace. I cling to this hope often when I feel like I am drowning in grief and sorrow and sadness. I cling to this image when my throat gets sticky, my chest is heavy, and it is hard to breathe.

In these moments, I have to stop and I see my twenty-one-year-old self in that orange plastic chair, the girl who was desperately hoping for a love like Grandma and Grandpa. I would tell her that finding that fierce love that smuggles pie into hospitals and dances next to death beds would mean a lot of heartache. I would tell her that she'd have one hell of a decade trying to grow up and settle down. I would tell her maybe she should have not asked a Costa Rican white water rafting guide to come join a Canadian adventure company during his winter months. Maybe she could have been a little more patient with Ronnie as we made our way to one another. I would tell her to savor the sweet, quiet moments rocking a baby in the early morning. And I'd tell her she should've known there would be pain involved in building a life that is full of meaning, joy, and beauty. But even though I didn't know all the stupid or spontaneous decisions I would make along the way, the Jessica who sat in that orange plastic chair did know a little about the end she wanted. A love that lasts.

Having the end in mind is key to building something that lasts. Have you sat with your partner and truly dreamt of what this would look like? Hot Ronnie and I picture what it will be like in seventy years. When we are old and wrinkly—maybe not that wrinkly thanks to Botox, but wrinkly-*ish*. We are sitting on our brick porch in the dream home we built overlooking the mountains, sipping on my homemade sweet tea and embracing the space and time to breathe. Hot Ronnie often says when we fight, "You better figure this out Janzen, 'cause you are stuck with me for the next seventy years." He uses this line when I get so mad at him and can't seem to get my head wrapped around it. Yes, shocking, we still get mad at each other. But we do a hell of a lot better job getting through it and letting go. Maybe it is even a little silly, but imagining being old with Hot Ronnie puts things in perspective pretty damn fast. I go back to this vision of us decades from now: a simple life where others are welcome any time of the day, a home with a porch facing west so we can sit in peace and watch the sunset or drink hot French press early in the morning when no one else is around, and most importantly, a stubborn love that we both know will outlast anything life throws at us.

THE NUDGE:

When life gets hard, it is tempting to just throw in the towel, especially in marriage or a partnership. But I encourage you to follow the nudge that tells you to water the grass where you are. Follow the nudge to stay, to show gratitude, to find ways to better be there for the people you love. Life can get really hard, and it's chaotic and moving 1,000 miles per hour, but follow the nudge to pause, to actually work through things that feel off, to honestly communicate.

THE CHOICE:

You get to choose whether or not to water your grass. You get to choose to see your spouse as an enemy or an ally. You get to choose whether or not to invest in a future with them, cast a vision with them, support them in the most trying seasons, share a piece of pie with them. Investing in your marriage and choosing to see through eyes of gratitude (instead of focusing on the shit) takes work. But you aren't in it alone. You have a teammate to help you water the grass.

THE JOY:

The joy comes from not giving up, from saying "Look at what we accomplished together." The joy comes from having hard and honest conversations at marriage conferences, changing what needs to change, and doing the work. The joy comes from stubborn love—love that is lasting and steadfast. Love that always brings the joy.

Conclusion

CHIPS ALL IN

*the nudge to write a book
and make a dream a reality*

Play the hell out of the hand you are dealt—chips all in.

Maybe, just maybe, my story relates to you. Maybe you had a miscarriage or lost a young baby. Maybe you have grieved the loss of a child or not being able to have children. For that, I am so sorry. I don't get why life happens the way it does for some of us. No parent should outlive their kid; no one should be denied to be a parent if it is all they dream of becoming. Maybe you're not facing the loss of a child, but crippling anxiety, depression, job loss, marriage failure, financial upset, or the loss of a business, or the craziness of COVID-19. Maybe you are grieving the loss of a spouse, an idea, or a dream. Your life hasn't panned out in the way we are told the story should go. It hasn't been all you dreamed it would be. To you who are in darkness—you can change the darkness and find the light. You can be the light; you can overcome this. Read that again and write that down and write it daily until you believe it.

God has carved out this story for me—he has shaped me and molded me and nudged me toward joy, time and time again. I would not have chosen to write my story this way, trust me, but it is how my story is written. Though we don't get to choose the cards we are dealt, we all get the chance to choose how we play them and respond. I get a choice in how I live and, most importantly, respond. As my mama always says, "Everything is redeemable." And as the wise and incredibly driven Marie Forleo says, "Everything is figure-outable."

We all have nudges on our heart, and mine has been to write a book for over six years. This was just supposed to be a crazy love story about the nudges of my heart to reach out to the hot guy at work. But now, it is even bigger than that. There is so much more to the story. The nudge to write this book has been years in the making. Often, I have been so frustrated and discouraged because it didn't happen faster. I have beaten myself up way too many times because it wasn't done.

It has taken faith and discipline to complete this massive project. Committing to writing this story meant missing out on activities and events and fun things with my kids or hubby sometimes. It meant setting an alarm and getting up earlier than everyone else to find quiet time. I started writing this book in 2014, and lot of life happened from that time to today. As long overdue as this book feels, I also know that it is coming into the world just at the right time. *Bring the Joy* is for right now.

I can't finish this book without telling you how the fact that you're holding it in your hands was the result of paying attention to a nudge. In 2017, two of my best friends took me to Los Angeles. It was a last-minute trip to get out of the city. I needed a change of scenery after Lewiston's passing, and they made it a priority to make the trip happen. We gathered and made sticky notes of all the activities we wanted to do. One of mine was to attend a church service at Zoe.

Our first morning in LA, we hit up a spin class, ate an overpriced brunch, and then went to grab a coffee. We picked this total hipster LA coffee place, and I have no idea why because one of my friends almost exclusively drinks Starbucks Vanilla Lattes with lactose-free milk. Anyway, we walked up to the shop, and the wall had a mural with a massive lion on it. When I see lions, I always think of Lewiston, my little fighter. I always try and pay attention to little things that remind me Lewiston is still around. When we landed at the airport and got into the cab, "Can't Stop the Feeling!" came on the radio. We call it Lewiston's song. I felt that familiar tug as I always do.

Inside the coffee shop, I swear I spotted Chad Veach—the pastor of Zoe Church. If you don't know Chad, he is the pastor of a church in Los Angeles, and his daughter is terminally ill. When I was in Hawaii, I had finished reading his book, *Unreasonable Hope,* and I found great comfort in his family's story. I had been following him on social media and knew it was him. I tried to search on Instagram to see if he had posted where he was having coffee (I mean, talk about creepy), but between staring at him and my phone, we made eye contact. He could totally tell I was checking him out. And not in a weird way, but in a "Do I know you?" way.

I walked right up to him and asked point blank, "Are you Chad Veach?" Sure enough.

I went into this whole story about reading his book, losing my son Lewiston, getting a tattoo here in LA of the words "Run Towards the Roar," which is one of the chapter titles of his friend Levi Lusko's book *Through the Eyes of a Lion.* (Levi lost his daughter to an asthma attack right around Christmas). I had also just finished that book and it moved me to the core. Clearly enough to tattoo it on my forearm as a daily reminder to Run Towards the Roar—it means run towards the things that scare you the most. Chad graciously offered to FaceTime Levi Lusko so I could show him my tattoo. I told Chad I was planning to go to his church the next day as well. He gave us the low down and made sure we were taken care of. The next morning, we attended his service. As I was leaving the church, I thanked him for his time and asked him if he had any suggestions or tips for writing a book.

"Do you have an agent?" he asked.

I didn't, I replied, and he offered to send an email to his agent. A month or so later, I had a phone call with the Fedd Agency. Later that summer Hot Ronnie surprised me with a trip for my birthday to Austin, Texas to meet the Fedd team where I made a personal visit to their office, and later signed a contract to publish this book.

Friends, let me tell you: it has not been for the faint of heart. It has taken sacrifice and some divine intervention to make it happen. But with persistence and consistency, this book is now my reality and in your hands. So, trust the process. Do the work, be prepared for six years not six weeks of work. We are so used to Amazon Prime next day delivery that sometimes we forget that it doesn't happen over night. Trust those nudges because the nudges lead to the good work being done.

My next nudge? Become a New York Times bestselling author, find a cure for SMA, and travel the world speaking on stages and sharing my story. Oh, and a bonus is being a guest on Good Morning America. Casual, right?! Dream big is my motto. I used to care what people thought of me and my dreams. And finally—*finally*—I have learned to not care one damn bit. Judge away, Susie; it's a good thing I don't care what you think because I am staying in my lane and working my butt off to build the best life possible for my family.

Losing Lewiston was my wake-up call.

You know when you're driving and your phone beeps? For a brief second, you look down, just to look to see who it was . . . oh don't judge, we have all done it. (My car still has a tape deck in it so there is no bluetooth connection, okay.) The phone rings, and you glance down for but a second. When you look up, the car in front of you has slammed on the brakes, and you must do the same. You slam on your brakes and your heart is racing because you are inches from hitting the car in front of you. BOOM. YOU'RE AWAKE. The wake-up call to PAY ATTENTION. That's where I was: heart racing, seconds away from crashing because I wasn't listening to those nudges. Today, I am awake and alert, I am tuned into those nudges.

Part of what Lewiston taught me was that every single day of life matters. They say the average person gets 30,000 days. Lewiston was gifted 179. He lived his days well, and you know why he lived those days well? Because we lived life on purpose, for a purpose. You tend to live life a bit differently when death is knocking at your front door. You tend to breathe a little deeper, take more risks and chances, and say yes to the amazing opportunities in front of you. Are you really going to wait for death to knock at your door before you jump all in and follow that nudge?

Do you need a life-or-death moment to wake you up, shake you, and catapult you into living fully and seeking the change you need? I don't think I was living terribly, but I was coasting and comfortable. Most of us are. In the wise words of Rachel Hollis, "I was MADE FOR MORE," and so are you! So do the thing, make the change, and take the leap. Fly, soar, and reach for everything you dream of. The ground underneath you will not always be firm. It *will* get steep and slippery, there will be hurdles but you just need to keep stepping forward, embracing the suck, the joy, and all the challenges. It will pay off. I promise. Follow that nudge, that ache in your heart for more. Those nudges will bring you joy.

The day that death knocks at my front door, I want to greet it with arms wide open and say, "Take me because I lived well, I lived with all I had, and I didn't hold back." Hot Ronnie and I often talk about his overdose—we talk about what it was like lying face down on the floor, knowing that this was pretty much the end for him and still he begged God for one more chance. I thank God every day that I have a husband who has fought so hard to make changes in his life because I know he's never just going to coast. He isn't going to take for granted the breath in his lungs and the movement in his legs and the beat of his heart. He isn't going to hope that one day, all will be right. He is going to go after his life and his dreams, take all his vitamins daily, and give it all he has. That is what inspires me and moves me: opportunity for more.

If I look at where my life was when I married Hot Ronnie, to when I had my first two kids, to now—Holy Hannah, it is crazy. Like Hot Ronnie promised me after our run that one stormy night, with him, the mountaintops seem higher. We still have valleys but we face them together as a team. Transformation didn't just happen overnight. Change has happened because we have shown up time and time again, and progress has taken place. We have gotten off track, been distracted, and tried to outrun the pain. We had another healthy baby—his name is Hollis. And yes, we named him after Rachel and Dave Hollis and the life-changing work that their whole company is doing. Call me crazy or obsessed, I don't care. That work has changed my life. I am better for it; we are better because of it. We have become stronger as a couple, we continue to fight for joy.

In Lewiston losing his life, I have found mine. It is probably the best and the worst thing that has happened to me and to us as a couple. And yes, it is really hard to write that sentence. My life forever changed because of that little lion. I can confidently say that even after losing my son—my precious babe—and having our world totally rocked by financial lows, losing Ronnie's dad, almost getting divorced, quitting what I thought was my dream job with a big salary and walking away with no plan or direction, I am living my life with all that I've got. I am FULL, FREE, AND FILLED WITH SO MUCH JOY. Truly living the dream. I will let nothing hold me back. I will run towards my roar.

May this story be a small beacon of light to nudge you to live the most joyful yet.

The nudges aren't always wild ideas like raising a million dollars for your foundation or writing a New York Times bestseller, or chasing after the hot guy in the office. They are often the small things like telling that person they are loved, holding that door open for the elderly lady, calling your mom to say I love you, smiling and making eye contact with the stranger passing by, going to visit a friend that has been on your heart, praying for whoever comes to mind right then and there. Bringing a coworker coffee, inviting a friend to church, being bold in your opinion even when it isn't comfortable, quitting the job that isn't right, going for a run because your legs can move. Chasing after what excites you, traveling, exploring, taking the long way home, going left when you have always gone right, wandering through a neighborhood because you can, laughing at the mess (still working on this one), and dancing in the kitchen (or the hospital room) with or without music.

Find good people to journey with, and get into community so that when you don't have the strength to rise up again, someone will extend a hand, or put you on their back, or take the next step for you. *Do those things. Don't wait, don't hesitate! Do them right now.* Embrace the chaos, and stop trying to have it all perfect. This is life. *We aren't supposed to always know the next step; it is not always perfect.* We aren't just supposed to follow a checklist, although I do love a checklist. Life is all about figuring things out—nudge by nudge. Life is navigating and making mistakes and getting back up and trying something else out. Get good at not only noticing the nudges of your heart but choosing to respond to those nudges. Because that, my friend, is where the joy is. That is how you bring the joy!

THANK YOU'S

These thank you's are in no particular order, and they truthfully stressed me out. I am sure I am missing someone. Please don't be mad. I truly am doing the best I can.

First and foremost, I would like to thank the reader. This book is for you. If you made it all the way through, thanks for sticking it out. Thanks for turning the pages. My hope and desire is that you are moved to live a more full, authentic, unstuck life that brings the joy daily! Dream big, my friend, bigger than you ever thought possible—and go after it. Life is short. My prayer is that you don't need to wait till losing someone to fully let the chains and lies go that have held you back. I pray you become all you were created to be.

Let's be honest: this book would not have been possible without the amazing team at the Fedd Agency. From Jill to Tori to Allison to Ms. Fedd herself, thank you. I joked that this book should say written by Jessica and co-authored by Tori because she is that good. When I couldn't get the idea quite right on paper, she took what was swirling in my head and got it onto the lines of these pages. From start to finish, it has been almost three years to get to this point, and there is no other team I would have wanted to do it with. You saw my vision and my heart and you breathed life into it. Your dedication to this project and getting it just right means more than I can ask for. Thank you.

To anyone who purchased in the presale campaign and who

follows me on Instagram. Your support, love, posts, and encouraging words have kept me going. Strangers on the internet turn into friends because you witness our lives and the work we do and cheer us on. Grateful, thankful, and blessed just don't seem like big enough words. The book made it this far because you shared it or bought a copy. I am so thankful for social media and all the good it does.

To any clients that have hired me for "influencer" work—thank you. Thank you for trusting me with your brand. Because of your contracts, I didn't have to go back to a 9:00-5:00 and have been able to live my dream out every day. I am honored that you chose me.

To all the members of the Love for Lewiston Board. You jumped all in, and to this day, you have not stopped giving of your time, talent, and treasure. You are world changers.

To Dr. Mah—you don't get enough credit. You still continue to journey with our family. Thank you for serving how you do.

To anyone who provided care to Lewiston. Our journey was much lighter because of you. I am in awe of the care you gave. You truly are angels that walk around with wings tucked in.

To all team members of the Alberta Children's Hospital Foundation. Thank you for always being so willing to honor Lewiston and help us do good work. I am so thankful we can partner together for good.

To my three fav ladies who photograph my life so I can post it for the world to see on the 'gram. Kara, you insisted on doing an actual photoshoot for the cover, and man, am I glad we did. You have been snapping me since 2017 when I decided to start my blog. You have shown up time and time again—you know where to place my chin and my hips, and you laugh everytime I do "the Jessica." Thank you for believing in me and this project and all the projects in between. You showed up at Lewiston's first birthday even though we had never met in person. I gave you no direction, and you gave it 100 percent. I am so thankful for you, your talent, and your friendship.

To Kristina and KristyAnne. You two are beauties. Juggling the crazy chaos, capturing births, writing songs, and being dear friends. Thanks for being willing to put on a swimsuit and shoot at a public pool and for always finding new adventures with the kids. Thank you for capturing footage of me on the toilet and understanding the vision regardless of how crazy the ideas are that I come up with. Thank you for cheering me on; your incredible friendship and constant prayers are needed and so felt.

To Heather Boersma—wow. From coffee shop dates as almost strangers to hopping on a plane four days after I asked you to help me with my book—you've always had my back. Thank you for helping me work through all the crazy thoughts in my head to finish my rough draft so I could begin the crazy editing process with the Fedd Agency. You are always up to help, listen, and cheer me on.

To Morgan MacDonald. In everything—including grocery runs, childcare, markets, folding clothing, or helping out with another idea—you are always there to lean on. Thank you.

To Sunny Britton. Thank you for keeping me on track, making me laugh, and correcting the grammar in my posts. Thank you. You believed in me when others said I wasn't good enough—thanks for seeing the spark and keeping it going rather than putting it out.

To Melissa Hryszko. What a blessing you are to my family. Thank you for your incredible support and constant care.

To Jennifer Principalli. I have longed for an assistant since I dreamt of being a CEO. I interviewed three people for the job, and you, well, you followed up with me eight times until I just couldn't say no. I have no idea how I lived with out you before. You're my secret weapon. I know this is only the beginning and I am beyond thankful because you do way more than I pay you to do. Please don't ever leave me. Thanks for being part of Team Jessica and all the crazy. You are incredible to be able to handle me and keep the wheels on. This book got published because you handled all details that no one sees. Thank you for following up eight times and continuing to follow up. You are the best.

To Roger Laing for giving me some of the best advice and always believing in me to do great things. If you ever see me use the quote "Dream big. Go anywhere. Do anything.", that is from Mr. Laing himself. Roger, thank you for believing in me and for taking me on a winter walk one night. Thank you for pulling me aside and saying that I don't need to be any other version of myself but Jessica Janzen. I am enough just as I am. That night sticks with me forever. I am so grateful to have someone as highly respected as you pour into my life. You saw something in me that I needed to believe in me.

To ALL my girls. Thank you for speaking life into me, praying for me, working out with me, having a glass of wine with me, suprising me with a sweat sesh, and most importantly, for seeing the vision and meeting me in the basement for year one of Lewiston's birthday and sticking with me ever since. Thank you for always showing up, supporting, attending, giving, and being excited for me and my dreams.

To Victoria. You helped me pack over 3000 books! You are the shipping master and I have mad respect. You are an incredible friend and helped me tame the negative self talk wheel and believe that anything is possible. Thank you for seeing me through the darkness and making sure I came out the other side stronger. Thanks for being my person, my shipper, and partner in crime for all things LFL related. You never expect anything in return and serve so beautifully. My goals and dreams are not possible without your brilliance and dedication. THANK YOU!

To Justine. You get me, and that is one of the greatest blessings anyone can ask for. Thanks for always jumping into the mess, ready to figure it out. Including coding my website, fixing my internet default browser, and always listening to my latest request even when you have more pressing projects. You have shown up for me since that coffee date after spin class, and I know I got you till we are old and gray.

To Kirsty. Thank you for your friendship, doing life together, and most importantly, starting the dance parties. It changed the direction of our lives forever and I have you and Allie to thank for that. And well, JT should be thanking you for making it a number one hit. Bless you.

To Laura White. You would dive through a dumpster with me even when we haven't seen each other in over a year and you only have a few hours to visit after you flew in just for a day because you were nudged to see me. Your friendship is the deepest and purest. You never expect anything in return. You are a gift and a blessing. I love you.

To my mastermind girls. I knew our group was something special but had no idea how much I would be blessed by you. Thank you for always making time for all my crazy questions and challenges and giving me a new way to think about it. You have celebrated so many moments with me in my business and I am constantly in awe of your support.

To Laura Brows. The first time I met you, you scared me—you were intimidating. But now I know you, and how you only want the best for me. Thank you for your generosity, reshaping my brows so they aren't stuck in the '90s, and for giving me opportunities. Your coaching and encouragement have made me better. Thank you for consistently having my back and investing in me.

To Jodie. You truly came out of nowhere. You opened up your home to me and my mom. You see a need and you find a way to fill it. From home baked goods, to visits, to hot coffees and my fav gluten free muffins, you just don't stop. Beyond grateful. Thank you.

To Ishan, Shanaya & Karen. You changed my heart and expanded my world in ways I did not know possible. Thank you for being such incredible teachers of joy in the midst of your fight against SMA. I will work till we find a cure.

To Jonathan and Natasha Lambert, our pastors at Experience Church. We sought you out for prayer and a miracle the first Sunday we attended EC. From that meeting in the hallway, you have graciously journeyed with our family through all seasons of life. Thank you for serving and showing up as you do not only for us but for the community. I am constantly in awe of what you have built and continue to build. We are blessed to call you friends.

To all of Ronnie's grandparents that love me like I am their own granddaughter. Thank you for never making me feel like an in-law.

To my MIL. Thank you for cheering me on, and helping with endless amounts of childcare. What I do is not possible with out your help. You love your grandkids so much.

To Tanner and Lexie—I know I am at lot to handle, but I think after all these years, you get me. Thank you for showing up and loving me like a sister.

To my grandparents. Although none are living, I know you were waiting at Heaven's gate to greet Lewiston with open arms. Thank you for the gift of faith. What a blessing. I only hope I can raise my kids the same way.

To Joe and Sarah—thank you for believing in the work we are doing and always supporting us, even if it means flying across the country to cheer us on.

To my little brother Billy. The world is a better place with you in it. Whatever girl ends up marrying you is one lucky lady, because you are a catch and a half. Thanks for being so easy going and helping me see my projects come to life.

To my mom and dad. I know I drive ya crazy. Just think of how dull life would be if I wasn't there pushing you and the rest of the family along. Mom, I know you have believed in me always, I am constantly covered in prayer because you spend so much time on your knees. Thank you for always being there at a drop of a hat, for staying weeks and months with us to make it all okay and allow our world to go round. You are the silent hero who doesn't get enough credit. You are a blessing. I am so thankful God gave me you as my mom. Thanks for keeping me grounded and giving me the wings to fly. Dad, I know you love me even if I don't think you say it enough. You're quiet and steady and patient and will take my call at anytime no matter what is going on. Thank you for always being there no matter how silly it seems. I love you both so much. I am proud to call you my parents, and so thankful for the loving example that both of you set—forty years of marriage. Thanks for making sure Hot Ronnie and I never threw in the towel and for seeing us through.

To my children—Swayzie, Lewiston, and Hollis, and whoever else God will bless us with one day. When you are old enough to read these words, I pray that they inspire you so you know that anything is possible. You are the greatest joys in this life. Watching you learn and explore is such a privilege, and I treat it as such. I can't believe God blessed me with you. I can't wait to watch you do your thing, pursue your dreams, and follow the nudges of your heart. I love you more than you will ever know.

To my hubby, Hot Ronnie. Thank you just isn't enough. We have had so much joy in the journey. I had no idea it would be this hard, this challenging, and add this much additional crazy to our lives. I am wild and never like to do anything the easy way. God made you extra special to be able to put up with me. Thank you from the bottom of my heart for doing life with me the way you do. You are constantly serving me. You never make it about you, but simply give me the space and the freedom I need to go after my big, wild ideas. Thank you for putting the kids down so I could write or attend yet another event. You stayed back so I could go do what I needed to do to make my dream a reality. What a blessing it was to be nudged to go after you. What a blessing to follow the nudges to keep confessing my undying love. I knew you would eventually get there, even if it wasn't as fast as I wanted. What a blessing to get to journey and do life with you. There is no one I would rather do it with. I am truly living out my dream life, not just chasing it but truly living it, and it is because of you and your unwavering love. I love you, Hot Ronnie, and can't wait to be eighty and grey and on our back porch facing west, soaking it all in and reminiscing about all the incredible nudges we have had together. I couldn't ask for a better hubby, father to our kids, partner, and soulmate. Thankful to bring the joy with you!

ABOUT THE AUTHOR

Jessica Janzen Olstad is a motivational speaker, author and a 'serial-preneur'. She and her husband Hot Ronnie are the founders of the Love for Lewiston Foundation and small business owners. After losing their son Lewiston in 2016, Jessica decided that she would stop wasting time and get moving on her big dreams—speaking, writing and inspiring others to just go for it. Her clothing line, The Lewiston Label, highlights the life lessons Lewiston taught her. She loves a great cup of hot coffee in her favorite mug, spending time with her family and friends, checking out new restaurants with her Hot Hubby for date night, soaking up sunshine, traveling and adventures on the water, preferably wake surfing or paddle boarding.

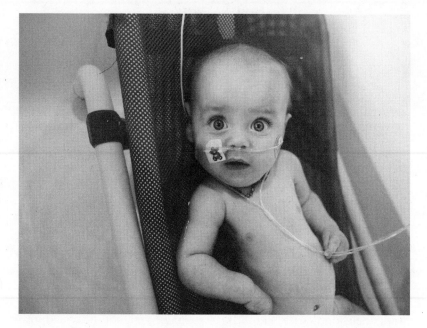

LEWISTON JAMES OLSTAD
May 25, 2016 – November 22, 2016

ABOUT THE
LOVE FOR LEWISTON
FOUNDATION

The Love for Lewiston Foundation was born when the Olstads decided to spend their son Lewiston's first birthday not as a pity party, but a celebration of his short but influential life. They felt the community surround them in their darkest moments and encountered so much light and strength in sharing their burden that they wanted to keep bringing joy and spreading love to others as it was so generously given to them. They believe to their core that Lewiston's message of "squeezing a little tighter, loving a little deeper, and dancing a little longer" is meant to be extended to the world.

To date, the Love For Lewiston Foundation has raised over $1,000,000 since starting on May 25, 2017. The Foundation is impacting lives across Canada and financially supporting critical research and medical needs for families fighting Spinal Muscular Atrophy and The Alberta Children's Hospital Foundation and Rotary Flames Hospice where Lewiston was cared for and then passed. The founding pillars will always be to CHOOSE MOVEMENT, BRING JOY & SPREAD LOVE. If you feel nudged please head to www.loveforlewiston.ca to learn more or support.

For every book sold $2.50 will be donated back towards LFL and the critical work it continues to do.

GET CONNECTED:

@thejessicajanzen | jessicajanzen.ca
@loveforlewiston | loveforlewiston.ca
@thelewistonlabel | thelewistonlabel.ca